CONTENTS

Ships in Focus Publications

Correspondence and editorial:
Roy Fenton
18 Durrington Avenue
London SW20 8NT
020 8879 3527
rfenton@rfenton.demon.co.uk

Orders and photographic:
John & Marion Clarkson
18 Franklands, Longton
Preston PR4 5PD
01772 612855
shipsinfocus@btinternet.com

Printed by Amadeus Press Ltd., Cleckheaton,
Yorkshire.
Designed by Hugh Smallwood, John Clarkson
and Roy Fenton.
SHIPS IN FOCUS RECORD
ISBN 978-1-901703-86-3

SUBSCRIPTION RATES FOR RECORD

Readers can start their subscription with
any issue, and are welcome to backdate it to
receive previous issues.

	3 issues	4 issues
UK	£24	£31
Europe (airmail)	£26	£34
Rest of the world (surface mail)	£26	£34
Rest of the world (airmail)	£31	£41

SHIPS IN FOCUS
July 2008

If this editorial reads like a plug for Ships in F
the intention. It is, in fact, an editorial in prai
general.

An aspiring author who approached us recently, rejected our terms
for publishing his book citing 'recent advances in self-publishing' as a reason
for deciding to produce his own book. Sadly, efforts we have seen recently
hardly support the notion that self-publishing has moved forward. True,
there have been developments in *technology*, including cheap but reasonably
effective scanners and some progress towards 'print-on-demand' that allows
production to be adjusted in line with sales. But technological advances
are nothing without the skills that an editor and/or publisher brings to the
publication process. And what we have not seen is any improvement in the
editorial standards of self-published works; indeed, some recent examples
plumb new depths of incompetence.

The relationship between an author and an editor or publisher should
be a symbiotic one, to borrow a biological term: neither can live to the full
without the other. The author brings the idea, the research and the desire
to have his work in print. The publisher offers the conviction that the book
will command sufficient sales to make it worthwhile, brings the marketing
and distribution resources to achieve those sales and – of most importance to
this discussion – insists on standards of research, writing style, presentation
and consistency that maintains his and the author's reputation. For a
publisher's standing is a pearl of great price and he needs to guard it jealously.
Reputation is won by convincing customers to buy his or her book and
ensuring that they are pleased with it and with subsequent productions. Once
lost it is hard to regain: one turkey might be forgiven, but not two.

Perhaps there are new authors out there who know it all, and can
self-publish a near-perfect book. But we have yet to meet one. Indeed, our
own individual introductions to the subtle arts of authorship and publishing
benefited enormously from help and advice of others with experience, not to
mention from some mistakes.

We wish the aspiring author well with his book, the subject of which
sounds a worthy one. We only hope that he has someone who can review
the standard of his research and presentation, and that he has the necessary
resources and skills to source photographs, design the book, supervise the
artwork and printing, market the finished product, warehouse his stock, handle
orders and despatch books to his customers. If he can do all these well, he
will have succeeded as a publisher.

John Clarkson   Roy Fenton

Moss Hutchison's *Melita* of 1971, photographed by W.D. Harris in the Bristol
Channel. See pages 206-7. *[J. and M. Clarkson]*

MOSS HUTCHISON: Part 2
Geoff Holmes, John Cook and Roy Fenton

Former Coast Lines' ships

ESNEH
Swan, Hunter and Wigham Richardson Ltd., Sunderland, 1919; 1,928g, 290 feet
T. 3-cyl. by Richardsons, Westgarth and Co. Ltd., Sunderland
In 1922 the Moss Steamship Co. Ltd. did a deal with Coast Lines Ltd., which was also part of the Royal Mail Group. The deal involved Moss exchanging their Caledon-built wartime standard ship *Limoges* (1,390/1919) for two slightly larger steamers which had also been laid down for the Shipping Controller. Seen in the top photograph, *Western Coast* was renamed *Esneh* (middle), and gave long service, sold only in 1948 when replacement motor ships had begun to arrive. She steamed on, first under Cypriot registry as *Tefkros* and later as the Hong Kong owned and registered *Shun On*. She was broken up in Hong Kong during 1959.

The name Esneh comes from the site of a temple on the Nile. *[Both: B. and A. Feilden/J. and M. Clarkson]*

ETRIB
Swan, Hunter and Wigham Richardson Ltd., Sunderland, 1919; 1,943g, 290 feet
T. 3-cyl. by Richardsons, Westgarth and Co. Ltd., Sunderland
The second of the Coast Lines ships transferred, *British Coast,* was originally intended to be named *War Shannon*. As Moss Hutchison's *Etrib* (bottom) she was not to be as fortunate as her sister, and on 14th June 1942 was torpedoed and sunk by the German submarine *U 552* in the North Atlantic. She was on a voyage from Cartagena to Liverpool in Convoy HG.84 with a cargo of apricot pulp, wine and cork. Four of her crew of 40 were lost, others being picked up by the corvette HMS *Marigold*, although one doubly unfortunate survivor spent an incredible 75 days on a raft before being picked up by a U-boat and made a prisoner-of-war. *[J. and M. Clarkson]*

Acquisitions from United Africa

MEROE

Barclay, Curle and Co. Ltd., Glasgow; 1929; 3,832g, 331 feet
T. 3-cyl. by Barclay, Curle and Co. Ltd., Glasgow

This steamer was built as *Lafian* for the African and Eastern Trade Corporation Ltd., but soon after completion she became part of the fleet of the newly-created United Africa Co. Ltd. Although the youngest ship in this fleet, she was not retained long, and in 1935 was sold to Moss Hutchison to be renamed *Meroe* (top). Her name came from an ancient city on the Nile north east of Khartoum.

Meroe was returning from Malta to the United Kingdom at the time Italy entered the war in 1940, and for the next five years she worked in the Eastern Mediterranean and Red Sea, not returning to Liverpool until November 1945.

Once new motor ships began to be delivered after the war, *Meroe* was sold to Germany where in 1950 she was renamed *Adele*, later becoming *Tucana*, and *Ursula*. In 1960 she was sold east, becoming successively *Mien An*, *Ruhamah* and finally *Liby*, as which she was broken up by Mollers Ltd. at Hong Kong in 1968.
[J. and M. Clarkson]

KYRENIA

Barclay, Curle and Co. Ltd., Glasgow, 1925; 3,543g, 322 feet
T. 3-cyl. by Barclay, Curle and Co. Ltd., Glasgow

In 1935 *Kyrenia* was also bought from United Africa for whom she had been built as *Nigerian* (bottom), but was not retained long by Moss Hutchison, being sold to Bristol City Line in 1937 to become *Toronto City*. *Kyrenia* took its name from a port in northern Cyprus. As related in 'Record' 33, where she was illustrated, *Toronto City* and her entire complement were lost in July 1941. No photos of her as *Kyrenia* are known. *[Roy Fenton collection]*

General Steam transfers

CHLORIS (2)

Ailsa Shipbuilding Co. Ltd., Troon, 1910, 1,180g, 240 feet
T. 3-cyl. by Ailsa Shipbuilding Co. Ltd., Troon

The 27-year old *Corncrake* (top), transferred from parent General Steam to Moss Hutchison in 1937, was hardly a gift, but *Chloris* as she became was to prove a survivor (middle). No sooner had she come through the war than in September 1945 she caught fire, capsized and sank in Trieste Harbour while loading empty petroleum drums. It took nine months to refloat her, and she was then declared a constructive total loss, but such was the need for ships in post-war Italy that she was repaired and put back into service in 1948 as *Sarga*. She was sold and renamed *Gianandrea* in 1953, and only at the mature age of 45 was she sent to the breakers at Savona in 1955. *[Roy Fenton collection; John Cook collection]*

PHILOTIS

Ailsa Shipbuilding Co. Ltd., Troon, 1926; 880g, 221 feet
T. 3-cyl. by Ailsa Shipbuilding Co. Ltd., Troon

The second General Steam vessel transferred in 1937 was the *Grebe* which became the second *Philotis* (bottom). At this stage traditional Hutchison names were still being used, a practice discontinued after

the Second World War. The year 1940 was the worst in Moss Hutchison's history, and *Philotis* was the second loss by collision that year, sinking on 3rd September after striking the Polish steamer *Lublin* (1,409/1932) near St. Goven's Light House when bound from Swansea to Lisbon with coal and general cargo. *[B. and A. Feilden/J. and M. Clarkson]*

LORMONT (2)

Greenock Dockyard Co., Ltd.,
Greenock, 1927; 1,561g, 241 feet
T. 3-cyl. by J.G. Kincaid and Co.
Ltd., Greenock

The third of the pre-war General
Steam transfers was *Woodcock*
(right), renamed *Lormont* in 1939
after a suburb of Bordeaux.
She looked distinctly smarter in
Moss Hutchison livery (below).
In May 1940 she brought back
over one thousand troops from
Dunkirk, and was also involved
in the evacuation of St. Malo.
Her career was again tragically
short, and she became the third
loss by collision in 1940, sinking
on 7th December after striking
the armed trawler HMS *Cortina*
in the Humber where *Lormont*
was serving as a guard ship.
Note the Leith registration on the
photograph of *Woodcock*. [*Ships*
in Focus; B. and A. Feilden/J. and
M. Clarkson]

Seven post-war near-sisters

During the Second World War Moss
Hutchison Ltd. lost eight of the 18
ships it had owned in 1939 and, with
some of the surviving steamers being
over 25 years old in 1945, renewal
of the fleet was vital. Responsibility
for designing the new ships was
given to the long-serving marine
superintendent, Capt. L.H. des
Landes who had joined the company
in 1917 (his first command was the
Landes (I) in the Bordeaux trade!)
Berths were booked during the war
with Harland and Wolff and William

Pickersgill so that work could begin
soon after hostilities ended and this
enabled Moss Hutchison to get early
delivery of the first three vessels. The
Memphis cost just under £365,000
when delivered in December 1947
but post-war demand for tonnage
was so high that by March 1952, the
Tabor from Caledon at Dundee cost
£573,000, an increase of 57%. The
ships were representative of current
shipbuilding practice, incorporating
a certain amount of welding, but
were technically undistinguished.
However, with a service speed of
14 knots they were an improvement

over the pre-war motors ships *Kheti*
and *Kufra* which, like many Pirrie-
Kylsant products, were considerably
underpowered and could manage only
11 knots.

The Arab nations' embargo
on trade with Israel meant that the
fleet was split into two. *Memphis*,
Karnak and *Tabor* traded to Haifa and
Tel Aviv/Jaffa and were blacklisted in
Arab ports. The other ships traded
to Egypt, Libya, Syria and Lebanon.
All the ships called at Cyprus, Malta
and Turkish ports. Papayanni, Prince
Line and other companies also had to
divide their fleets in this way.

KANTARA

Harland and Wolff Ltd., Belfast, 1947;
3,213gt, 366 feet
Burmeister & Wain-type 4SCSA
6-cylinder oil engine by Harland and
Wolff Ltd., Belfast

The post-war ships fell into three sub-classes. The first three delivered, *Kantara*, *Memphis* and *Karnak*, could be recognised by having inside working alleyways. This class also had a small hatch between number 2 hold and the bridge.

The first post-war motor ship, *Kantara* is seen, against a dramatic Bristol Channel sky and in Liverpool. Her name was taken from a castle built in the tenth century in the Kyrenia Mountains of Cyprus.

Kantara was the only one of this group of seven not sold to companies associated with D.N.

Leventakis, who traded under the name Grecomar Shipping Agency. Instead in 1972 she went to Adamantios and Mikes Bousses of Piraeus who registered her under the Cypriot flag as *Costantis II* in the ownership of the Adami Shipping Co. Ltd. A photograph of her by Malcolm Cranfield under this name appeared in 'Record' 38, page 119. *Costantis II* was broken up at Castellon in 1980. *[Both J. and M. Clarkson]*

MEMPHIS

William Pickersgill and Sons Ltd.,
Sunderland, 1947; 3,575gt, 365
feet
Doxford-type 2SCSA 4-cylinder oil
engine by North Eastern Marine
Engineering Co. (1938) Ltd.,
Wallsend-on-Tyne
Memphis was sold on 28th
April 1972 to Sifnonav Shipping
Company S.A., Panama
(Grecomar Shipping Agency Ltd.,
Piraeus, managers) and put under
the Greek flag as *Elias*. In 1981
she was sold to Fazal Corporation
Ltd. who began breaking her up at
Gadani Beach in December.

Situated just south of
modern Cairo, Memphis was the
ancient capital of Lower Egypt
from about 3000 BC to 2200BC.
According to some authorities
it was the largest settlement in
the world at this time. *[J. and
M. Clarkson; G.E.P. Brownell/
World Ship Society Ltd.; Fotoflite
incorporating Skyfotos]*

KARNAK
Harland and Wolff Ltd., Belfast, 1948;
3,198gt, 366 feet
Burmeister & Wain-type4SCSA
6-cylinder oil engine by Harland and
Wolff Ltd., Belfast
The 'solid' base of the superstructure distinguished the first three ships of the post-war programme. Sold in 1971 to the Leventakis company Keanav Shipping Co. Ltd., Panama, *Karnak* became *Eudocia* under the Greek flag. She went for breaking up in 1981.

Situated on the Nile close to the modern city of Luxor, Karnak is the site of the world's largest group of temples. The ship was photographed at Swansea (above). *[G.E.P. Brownell/World Ship Society Ltd.]*

AMARNA
Harland and Wolff Ltd., Govan, 1949;
3,422gt, 367 feet
Burmeister & Wain-type4SCSA
8-cylinder oil engine by Harland and
Wolff Ltd., Belfast
From *Amarna* the Moss Hutchison motor ships were delivered with a white hull (above). The chairman of both General Steam and Moss Hutchison at the time was Robert Kelso who took a personal interest in the ships of the group and particularly their crew accommodation. The last four vessels of the sextet, against everyone's advice, were given white hulls at his insistence. Much of the cargo handling in Mediterranean ports at the time was overside into lighters and the damage this caused to their paintwork gave the various chief officers much heartache. After Kelso's retirement the order was given for the ships to be repainted black when they next went

for overhaul, as the photographs of *Amarna* on this page show.

Demand for shipping space was so high when *Amarna* was delivered in July 1949 that freight receipts from her first voyage paid for her building cost of £451,191. *Amarna* and *Assiout* could be distinguished from the earlier three by having outside alleyways on the main deck port and starboard. This made them look larger than the earlier trio, although they were identical in size. Like the earlier three ships their

bridges were a continuation forward of the boat deck.

In 1967 *Amarna* was chartered to Cunard for service to the Great Lakes and renamed *Assyria* (bottom), reverting to her former name in 1968. On 9th October 1975 she was sold to Katianav Shipping Co. S.A., Panama and renamed *Kastriani III*, again under the Greek flag. In 1982 she went to Anglo Trading Co. Ltd., Gibraltar and was to have been renamed *Montrose* but was never registered under this name.

Sold again in 1984 to Haji Abdul Karim & Co., Pakistan she arrived at Gadani Beach in February 1984 and demolition began in March.

Amarna is on the site of various ancient settlements on the east bank of the Nile about 200 miles south of Cairo. Occupied subsequently by Romans and Christians, it took the name Amarna from a group of nomads who settled there in the 18th century. *[Opposite page: H.B. Christiansen; upper: Roy Fenton collection; bottom Ships in Focus]*

ASSIOUT

Harland and Wolff Ltd., Belfast, 1949; 3,422gt, 367 feet
Burmeister & Wain-type4SCSA 8-cylinder oil engine by Harland and Wolff Ltd., Belfast

Assiout was sold on 3rd August 1973 to Apolliananav Shipping Co. S.A. Monrovia and registered in Greece as *Chryssoula II*. She was seen at Port Said during May 1978 in a good state of maintenance. In 1981 *Chryssoula II* was sold to Admiral Ltd., Pakistan and arrived at Gadani Beach in November, demolition beginning the next month. *Assiout* and *Chryssoula II* were pictured in colour on page 227 of 'Record' 24.

      Assiout is a modern university town 230 miles south of Cairo. The name is a corruption of its old title, Syout. *[J. and M. Clarkson collection;]*

KYPROS

William Pickersgill and Sons Ltd., Sunderland, 1950; 3,499gt, 368 feet
Doxford-type 2SCSA 4-cylinder oil engine by North Eastern Marine Engineering Co. (1938) Ltd., Wallsend-on-Tyne

Kypros is seen in her natural habitat, the harbour at Malta (opposite page middle). Cyprus too might be considered home, as Kypros is the Greek name for the island, itself derived from the word for copper. The effect of adding an extra bridge deck and making the funnel much shorter gives her a rather different appearance to *Amarna* and *Assiout*, although she is of the same size.

Sandy Kinghorn's account of his time as a paint representative in 'Record' 27 brought to mind an incident when Geoff was a cadet on board *Kypros* at Famagusta. The mate had given the other cadet and him a 'job and finish' on a Saturday, painting the bridge dodgers and bulwarks (as cadets, rather than apprentices, they were entitled to overtime payments). The bosun had mixed a tasteful eau-de-nil and an early lunch had been arranged in the duty mess. By about 13.00 the cadets were finishing the job on the starboard side when the mate, having finished his lunch, erupted from the wheelhouse shouting 'What the **** have you two done – Oh! This side looks alright!' Following the mate to the port wing they found that the paint was drying in blue and white splotches. The bosun had mixed the then fairly new synthetic white gloss with a traditional oil-based green and the two types of paint had separated as they dried. The cadets got another 'job and finish' the following day. On seeing a Swedish ship with patches on her hull of the then new zinc chromate primer, another Moss Hutchison bosun was heard to say, 'That's what I was telling you about Mr. Mate, yellow red lead'!

In 1967 *Kypros* was chartered to Cunard for two voyages to the Great Lakes for which she was renamed *Aurania*. On 25th August 1976 she was sold to Keanav Shipping Co. S.A., Monrovia, registered in Greece and renamed *Angeliki*. In 1981 she was sold to Angel Shipping Co. Ltd., Malta and renamed *Angel* by simply painting out three letters. It was reported in April 1982 that she had been sold to breakers at Calcutta. *[B. and A. Feilden/J. and M. Clarkson collection; G.E.P. Brownell/World Ship Society Ltd.; W. D. Harris/Fotoship]*

TABOR

Caledon Shipbuilding and Engineering Co. Ltd., Dundee, 1952; 3,694gt, 385 feet
Doxford-type 2SCSA 4-cylinder oil engine by Hawthorn, Leslie and Co. Ltd., Newcastle-upon-Tyne

In the first photograph, a virginal white *Tabor* takes a deck cargo of buses into a Mediterranean port. In the second and third photographs she is seen in black. She was a development of *Kypros* with a longer and beamier hull. Distinguishing features include the slightly taller funnel and the longer open alleyway at main deck level. She was named after Mount Tabor, a few miles east of Nazareth in Palestine.

Tabor was chartered to the Admiralty around the time of the Suez crisis in 1956. The story goes that as she was entering Hong Kong she passed close to a Blue Funnel ship. The comment came across 'What happened? Did you forget to turn left at Gib?' *Tabor* also made one voyage to Guiana on charter to Booker Line in the summer of 1958.

On 12th September 1975 *Tabor* was sold to Apolliananav Shipping Co. S.A. to join the former *Assiout* under the Greek flag as *Katia*. In 1982 she was sold to Kate Shipping Co. Ltd., Malta and simply renamed *Kate*. Resold to Steel Industrials Kerala Ltd., India she arrived at Beypore to be demolished in March 1982.
[Roy Fenton collection (2); J. and M. Clarkson]

Post-war transfers

LORMONT (3)
Workman, Clark (1928) Ltd., Belfast, 1930; 936gt, 216 feet
T. 3-cyl. by Workman, Clark (1928) Ltd., Belfast

With Moss Hutchison's severe war losses, transfers from the General Steam fleet were necessary to supplement the building programme and to provide suitable smaller tonnage for the Liverpool and Glasgow to Bordeaux service. Thus in 1948 *Swift* became the third *Lormont* in just over a dozen years, although the top photo shows she was in Moss Hutchison colours before being renamed. With her counter stern, her hull looks more obsolete than that of her predecessor.

When sold in 1953 she pursued a familiar career, first sold to Greek owners who put her under Cyprus registry as *Silver Med*, then to Hong Kong owners in 1960 who altered her name to *Silver King*. Further renamings as *South Sea* and *Eugene* followed until she was broken up in Hong Kong in 1968.

Officially all vessels owned or chartered which were used on the old Hutchison services to France and Portugal flew the Hutchison flag as well as the Moss pennant (and not the ships on the Mediterranean service as we said in 'Record' 39), but photographs show that the practice was not always observed. These services were later run with chartered vessels and eventually succumbed to road transport after ro-ro ferries were introduced on the cross-channel routes. *[World Ship Society Ltd.; J. and M. Clarkson collection]*

LANDES
Greenock Dockyard Co., Ltd., Greenock, 1925; 893gt, 211 feet
T. 3-cyl. by Ross and Duncan, Glasgow

Hirondelle became *Landes* in 1949 (bottom), but served on the Bordeaux route for just four years. She was then sold to Italian owners who renamed her *Pilarella* and closed her shelter deck to increase her gross tonnage dramatically to 1,346. A further Italian owner renamed her *Turritania* until she was sold for demolition at Hamburg in 1961.

The name Landes was taken from forested area known as the Landes of Gascony west and south of Bordeaux. *[John Cook collection]*

KUFRA (2)

Caledon Ship Building and Engineering Co. Ltd., Dundee; 1937, 2,385gt, 315 feet
Oil engine 2SCSA 4-cyl. by Sulzer Brothers Ltd., Winterthur

At least eight other General Steam ships ran in Moss Hutchison colours in post-war years, but there was to be just one further formal transfer. General Steam had run a service from London to western Italian ports for many years but there was much competition and so they withdrew in 1956 and in September foisted the *Heron* (upper photo) on to Moss Hutchison for the inflated price of £110,000. As with the inflated charter rates paid by the subsidiary to its parent, this was a method of getting profits transferred to General Steam without having to pay tax on dividends. Moss Hutchison were having a buoyant trading period at the time and were without the *Tabor* but their new acquisition *Kufra* (lower photo) proved both expensive (£101,000 was written off her book value immediately she was purchased) and unsuitable as her small hatches were difficult for the stowage of large items then exported to the Levant. When trade dipped in 1959, by which time she was over 22 years old, the opportunity was taken to get rid of *Kufra* but she realised less than a third of what she had cost.

She was to have three further owners, all Greek but using three different flags. Pateras Brothers first named her *Arden* under Lebanese registry, then in 1965 Pothitos and Koutsofios put her under the Greek flag as *Sanmichael*. Final owners in 1967 were members of the Arnemakis family who in 1973 renamed her *Grand Michael* and moved her to Cyprus registry. Brodospas broke her up at Split, Yugoslavia in 1974. *[Geoff Holmes collection; Ships in Focus]*

Finale

On 1st October 1971, the Moss Hutchison ships came under the nominal management of P&O General Cargo Division. However, Moss Hutchison was still being run as an almost separate entity from offices in Water Street where one of the former directors, Tom Geddes, managed both the Mediterranean and the French/Peninsular services. Ownership remained unchanged until 18th April 1973 when *Amarna*, *Kypros* and *Tabor* plus two new ships *Melita* and *Makaria* were registered under the ownership of Peninsular and Oriental Steam Navigation Company. Because of the political situation in the middle east, the ships never painted up P&O's corporate livery nor were they given 'Strath' names: clearly, P&O did not want to risk antagonising Arab nations.

Disposal of the immediate post-war ships began with the sale of

Karnak in 1971, and was spread over five years, with *Kypros* not leaving the fleet until August 1976. It is remarkable that six of this group of seven were sold to the same Greek owner, D.N. Leventakis, who traded as Grecomar Shipping Agency Ltd. As the sales were spread over several years he was clearly not buying a job lot, and it must be assumed that Leventakis found the first ships he acquired to be very suitable for his Mediterranean trades and came back for more.

The Aberdeen pair, *Melita* and *Makaria*, were never satisfactory, having been built as stop-gaps before it was clear what was needed for the company's trades. Their engines also gave more than their fair share of problems. They were the last ships designed for Moss Hutchison, although a couple of Danish coasters were chartered to maintain the service for a few years. *Melita* and *Makaria* carried the black funnel with white band until the very end, although they had flown the P&O house flag, probably throughout their careers.

MELITA

Hall, Russell and Co. Ltd., Aberdeen, 1971; 2,686gt, 345 feet
Oil engine 4SCSA 14-cyl. by Crossley Premier Engines Ltd., Manchester
Although she was launched for Moss Hutchison, by the time *Melita* (opposite top) was delivered in December 1971, P&O General Cargo Division had taken over management of the fleet, and registration in P&O ownership followed in September 1973. She flew the P&O house flag, but retained the black funnel with white band until her sale, with her sister *Makaria*, in October 1979. Cargo gear in this pair of ships represented an upgrade over the previous generation of motor ships, with a 30-ton capacity Stülcken replacing the 25-ton conventional derrick, and two five-ton capacity deck cranes. The forward hatch was worked by a derrick-crane. Melita was the Latin name for Malta.

After only seven years' service, the last ships owned by Moss Hutchison were laid up in Liverpool during 1978. Sale in 1979 saw both ships go to Naviera Multinacional del Caribe S.A., a company set up in 1977 jointly by the governments of Costa Rica, Cuba, Mexico, Nicaragua, and Trinidad and Tobago. Its headquarters was in San Jose, Costa Rica but its three ships were registered in Panama. *Melita* was renamed *Siboney* and lasted another eight years, arriving at Tampico, Mexico in June 1987 to be broken up at the tender age of 16.

MAKARIA

*Hall, Russell and Co. Ltd., Aberdeen,
1972; 2,686gt, 345 feet
Oil engine 4SCSA 14-cyl. by Crossley
Premier Engines Ltd., Manchester
Makaria* (below) had a name not
previously used by Moss Hutchison,
and which was chosen to honour
Archbishop Makarios, first president
of the Republic of Cyprus, and not
regarded as friendly to the British
at the time when Cyprus was
gaining independence. On sale to
Naviera Multinacional del Caribe
S.A. in November 1979 *Makaria*
was renamed *Los Teques*, and like
her sister was broken up in 1987 at
Tampico, where she had been laid up
since 1985. This fine little cargo liner
thus traded for only 13 years.

BUSIRIS (2)

J.L. Thompson and Sons Ltd., Sunderland, 1961; 23,980gt, 691 feet
Two steam turbines double-reduction geared to a single shaft by Parsons Marine Turbine Co. Ltd., Wallsend-on-Tyne

Ordered immediately before the end of Moss Hutchison's financial year in 1957, the *Busiris* cost over £2,700,000 when she was delivered in March, 1961 almost as much as the whole of the rest of the fleet. Although she was managed by British India, and from April 1963 by the specially-formed Trident Tankers Ltd., the Moss directors had played a part in her design and got their reward when the net hire paid by Shell (almost £27,000 per month) started to contribute towards the company's profits: for example, in 1965-1966 she provided 64% of the voyage and trading results. A minor claim to fame was that at the time of her delivery *Busiris* was the largest vessel to have been built on the Wear.

Moss Hutchison ownership ended in October 1972 when *Busiris* was registered in the ownership of P&O. Her 15-year Shell charter came to an end in 1976 and she was quickly sold to breakers in Taiwan, who began work in August. The unfortunate shipbreakers got more than they had bargained for as, by the time she arrived at Kaohsiung, the considerable amount of sludge in her cargo tanks had set solid.

The name Busiris was that of an ancient Egyptian city on the Nile delta, and was also associated with a mythical king of Egypt. *[World Ship Society Ltd.; John Cook collection]*

Beginning a selection of colour photographs of Moss Hutchison ships, in their original and later colours, *Memphis* sails from Birkenhead on 17th June 1971 (above). She is seen again, almost exactly ten years later, as *Elias* passing Arnavutkoy on the Bosphorus: note the Turkish courtesy flag (below). Owners are now the Sifnonav Shipping Company S.A. of Panama and managers Grecomar Shipping Agency Ltd. of Piraeus, the trading name of D.N. Leventakis. Above the waterline, if not below, *Elias* looks remarkably smart for a ship that within six months will be sold to breakers. *[Paul Boot; Nigel Jones]*

Karnak at Cardiff on 20th April 1969 (top) and in Toxteth Dock, Liverpool on 12th May 1971 (middle) still flying the Moss Hutchison house flag from her main mast. Later in 1971 she was sold to the Leventakis company Keanav Shipping Co. Ltd. of Panama and became *Eudocia* under the Greek flag. She is seen well-laden off Port Said on 1st February 1978 (bottom). *[John and Andrew Wiltshire; Paul Boot; Mike Green]*

Amarna approaches Eastham and the entrance to the Manchester Ship Canal on 28th February 1975 (top). In October of the same year she became *Kastriani III* of the Katianav Shipping Co. S.A., Panama as which she wears Leventakis colours at Port Said on 1st February 1978 (middle). *[Paul Boot; Mike Green]*

Down to her marks is *Chryssoula II*, the former *Assiout*, passing Istinye in the Bosphorus in May 1981 under the ownership of Apollananav Shipping Co. S.A. of Monrovia (bottom). She had only a few months of life left, and was despatched to Gadani Beach in November 1981. *[Dave Salisbury]*

Angeliki of Keanav Shipping Co. S.A., Monrovia, the former *Kypros*, on the Bosphorus 24th April 1981 during her last full year in service (above). Like other Leventakis ships, she traded mainly in the Black Sea and the eastern end of the Mediterranean, almost all known photographs of the ships being taken there. *[Nigel Jones]*

Tabor was photographed in Harrington Dock, Liverpool on 13th November 1971 (below). Taken from the same angle as the slightly smaller *Angeliki*, the taller funnel of Tabor is apparent. *[Paul Boot]*

By now wearing P&O funnel colours, the tanker *Busiris* steams up the New Waterway on 18th September 1975 during her last year in service (above). *[World Ship Society Ltd.]*

The melancholy sight of *Melita* and *Makaria* laid up in Morpeth Dock, Birkenhead, awaiting sale on 14th April 1979 (below). They were sold in November of that year and went out to Central America. Ahead of them lies the classic Isle of Man turbine steamer *Mona's Isle. [Jim McFaul]*

VETERAN BRITISH-BUILT TUGS
Nigel Jones and Paul Boot

Although only very few of the once numerous ships built during the 1950s and 1960s survive today, there are a reasonable number of 'classic' diesel tugs from this era still active, particularly in the ports of Greece, Italy, Malta and Portugal. Those from British yards were built to a high standard by specialists such as Richard Dunston (Hessle) Ltd., and this proved a distinct advantage when the time came to sell. The purchasers appreciated their quality, which promised many more years of useful service, especially when they were assigned to light duties such as standing by during ship movements, handling ropes or pushing up against ships during berthing operations. This feature depicts a selection of British-built tugs, nearly all once familiar sights in UK ports, in their new guises.

NISOS KALYMNOS

The oldest by far of all the tugs illustrated is the former *Banco* (107/1927), built for Union Lighterage Co. Ltd. by Cochrane and Sons Ltd. In 1966 she was bought by Tsavliris (Salvage and Towing) Ltd. - one of no less than 25 former British tugs with which they built up their fleet around that time. *Nisos Kalymnos* was photographed at Piraeus in May 1972, a few years before she was sold to Nicolaos E. Vernicos for whom she became *Vernicos Katerina.* She was broken up locally in 1981. *[Dave Salisbury]*

ALFIOS

William Watkins' *Hibernia* (293/1963) was one of a pair of tugs built by Cochrane and Sons Ltd. at Selby to provide a significant fire-fighting capability on the Thames. The welded tubular-framed monitor tower rising above the open-topped bridge is an incongruous addition to this otherwise traditional company design. *Hibernia* was subsequently absorbed into the Alexandra Towing fleet and continued to serve them until sold to Greek buyers in 1987. As *Atrotos* and later *Karapiperis 10* she operated in the Piraeus area until 2006 when she was acquired by Katakolo Tug Services. Renamed *Alfios* after the river flowing past the ruins of Olympia down to the coast near the small port of Katakolon, she now attends the growing number of cruise ships calling there. Despite her age she is still in fine condition and when photographed just after sunrise in November 2006 her paint looked to be still wet. The company markings have since been added to the yellow upper section of the funnel. *[Paul Boot]*

HERAKLES

In 1958 Bristol Channel ship repairers C.H. Bailey Ltd. enterprisingly extended their trade abroad by taking over the Admiralty dockyard facilities at Malta. Trade was soon sufficiently brisk to justify ordering two sister tugs from the Atlantic Shipbuilding Co. Ltd. at Newport, Monmouthshire and they were completed in 1961 as the *Chris B* and *Sara B*. In 1967 both tugs were sold to other Maltese owners; the *Sara B* (140/1961) was renamed *St. Lucian*, which she held until 1981 when sold again and renamed *Gerit*. In 1982 she hoisted the Greek flag as *Poseidon III*, then became *Karapiperis III* in 1984 and finally *Herakles* in 1988. She was last reported at Thisvi in April 2007, but was based at Rhodes when photographed on 19th September 1990. The liner waiting to dock in the background is the Turkish *Akdeniz* (8,809/1956), which amazingly is still afloat, though now a training ship at Tuzla. *[Nigel Jones]*

LEON

Leon (290/1960), pictured on 17th September 2005 passing some of the ship repair facilities at Perama, was formerly *Anglegarth* ordered in 1958 by R. and J. H. Rea Ltd. but completed in April 1960 by Henry Scarr Ltd., Hessle for William Cory and Sons Ltd. to be managed by Rea. She was the third of four similar tugs by Scarr built to handle large tankers at Milford Haven, where Esso had invested in a new oil refinery and B.P. in a terminal for supplying their Llandarcy refinery near Swansea via a 60-mile buried pipeline. In 1963 she was transferred to ownership of R. and J.H. Rea Ltd. and in 1970 this company was restyled as Cory Ship Towage Ltd. Also in 1970 *Anglegarth* moved to Newfoundland for a spell, then in the mid-1970s was chartered to work in the West Indies and at Curacao. She returned to the UK in 1976 for duties at Avonmouth before sale in 1979 to Andreas & George Kyrtatas, Greece and renamed *Leon;* since 1983 registered owners have been Leon Maritime Co. *[Nigel Jones]*

MINOTAVROS

The prominent diamond on the funnel of *Minotavros* (174/1960) is a clue to the identity of her former British owners. She was completed by W.J. Yarwood and Sons Ltd. at Northwich as the *Plumgarth* for R. and J. H. Rea Ltd. Along with sister *Avongarth* she was based at Avonmouth, although a few years later *Plumgarth* was reallocated to Cardiff. In 1985 she was sold to Minos Shipping, Heraklion, who have made a few alterations, notably the removal of her flying bridge and lifeboat but added fire-fighting equipment. Photographed on 26th June 1993, *Minotavros* remains in regular service at Heraklion. *[Nigel Jones]*

DRITTO

None of the dozen steam powered tugs built post-war for Alexandra Towing had lengthy careers with the company but all but two of them found ready buyers in Italy. Converted to oil-burning in 1962, *Waterloo* (200/1954) lasted until 1972 when she was acquired by Societa Rimorchiatori Napelotani to join their large and mainly steam powered fleet at Naples. Not long after arriving at her new home port, *Dritto* is seen here at work in May 1972 with an interesting, but unfortunately unidentified, selection of the company's other steam tugs. In June 1989 she was dismantled by local breakers. *[David Salisbury]*

AGIA MARINA

With her twin uptakes, N.E. Vernicos's *Agia Marina* (147/1966), pictured near Salamis on 27th September 2004, bears a close resemblance to one of the diesel tugs operated by J.H. Lamey Ltd. on the Mersey in the 1960s. However, she is actually the former *Trafalgar* owned by Alexandra Towing Ltd.; ironically it was Alexandra who acquired the Lamey fleet in 1968. The *Trafalgar*, built by R. Dunston (Hessle) Ltd., was sold to Greek owners in 1992 and renamed *Megalochari VII*; she joined the Vernicos fleet in 1999. The Greeks have replaced her original funnel with the uptakes, an alteration that aesthetically is considered to have had a detrimental effect on her appearance. *[Nigel Jones]*

VERNICOS MARTIN

The *Vernicos Martin* (159/1960), completed by Cammell, Laird and Co. (Shipbuilders and Engineers) Ltd. at Birkenhead in 1960, makes a fine sight at full speed in the Great Harbour, Piraeus on 29th September 1990. Formerly *Flying Cock* of North West Tugs Ltd., operated and managed by Liverpool Screw Towing Co. Ltd., she was their penultimate new-building before they were acquired by Alexandra Towing in 1966. Renamed *Gladstone* in 1970 she remained on the River Mersey until 1981 when the last five of the former Cock tugs were sold to Nicolas E. Vernicos Shipping Co. Ltd., although only the *Flying Cock* and *Heath Cock* survived the delivery voyage. On transfer in 1994 to another Vernicos-owned company *Vernicos Martin* was renamed *Agios Andreas*. She was still in use during September 2004 and is listed by 'Lloyd's Register' in 2008. *[Nigel Jones]*

AGHIOS GERASSIMOS

In 1958 three new sister tugs were delivered to Johnston Warren Lines Ltd. for River Mersey duties, replacing three elderly steam tugs. The *Rossmore* was delivered by Charles Hill at Bristol, while the *Foylemore* and *Kilmore* were built by W.J. Yarwood and Sons Ltd. at Northwich. In 1968 the trio were acquired by Rea Towing Ltd. and, to bring them in line with the rest of their fleet, their names were tweaked in 1969 by changing the '-more' suffixes to '-garth'. In 1984 *Kilgarth* (208/1958) was sold to Loucas Matsas and Sons Shipping Co. Ltd., Greece and renamed *Aghios Gerassimos*. The photograph was taken on 30th June 1993 just after she had cast off her ropes from one of the ferry berths at Piraeus. In 1999 *Aghios Gerassimos* was sold to other Greek operators and in 2003 to North Korean-flag interests, being renamed *Hellas* and *Weisshaupt* respectively. She is still listed by 'Lloyd's Register' in 2008. *[Nigel Jones]*

CAPETAN GIANIS

The *Capetan Gianis* (199/59) is a fine example of the diesel tugs that P.K. Harris, Appledore built in the 1950/60s for various owners. Ordered by Rea Towing Company, Liverpool for River Mersey service, she was delivered as the *Willowgarth* in October 1959, following a few months after her identical sister *Hazelgarth* from the same yard. These were the first diesel tugs in the Rea fleet and their immediate success was to lead inevitably to the steam members disappearance a decade or so later. In 1985 *Willowgarth* was transferred to Cory Ship Towage Ltd, soon afterwards restyled Cory Ship Towage Ltd. The following year she was sold to Makedonia II Shipping Co (managed by Michael Gigilinis), Greece and renamed *Thisseas*. In 1988 ownership briefly passed to Thisseas Shipping Co. before sale to Evifan Towage-Salvage Shipping Co. and renamed *Capetan Gianis*. Pictured from a passing ferry at Heraklion on 26th June 1993, the elevated position clearly shows that her appearance has changed remarkably little over the years. She is still in service at Heraklion with Evifan, though before December 1997 her funnel colours were changed from yellow with red band to red with white band. Since 2005 registers have shown her as *Capetan Giannis*. [Nigel Jones]

AL HAMED

The civil engineering contractors John Howard and Co. Ltd. built up a small fleet of tugs in the late 1960s principally for towing barges of rock from North Wales to be used in the construction of Seaforth Dock at Liverpool. A couple of the vessels were secondhand purchases but they also ordered three new tugs from Richards (Shipbuilders) Ltd., at Lowestoft which were registered in Liverpool to their northern subsidiary company. All were sold on completion of the work in 1971 and *Elizabeth Howard*, together with her two sisters, passed to Gray, MacKenzie and Co. Ltd., and was put to work in the Middle East as *Al Hamed*, retaining British registry. Following an internal transfer in 1981 she was renamed *Grayotter* and a series of later sales to local owners saw her become *Sea Gull*, *Kanhaiya* and *Shaima 2*. Sporting a very weary red ensign and a line of drying washing, *Al Hamed* is seen at Dubai in February 1978. [Mike Green]

POLIKOS

With painting of her hull well in progress, Portolos Hellenic Tugboats' *Polikos* (198/1962) was photographed 29th July 1998 at Thessaloniki, the principal port of northern Greece. She was completed by T. Mitchinson, Gateshead as the *Cultra* for J. Cooper (Belfast) Ltd. and based in Northern Ireland for 18 years. In 1969 R. and J. H. Rea Ltd purchased Coopers and the following year she was transferred to the subsidiary Cory Ship Towage (N.I.) Ltd. In 1980 she moved to the Bristol Channel for service at Newport until 1983 when she was sold to her final British owners Frank Pearce (Tugs) Ltd. of Poole and renamed *Pullwell*. However, she did not to last long with Pearce, and moved to Greece in 1985. She is still listed by 'Lloyd's Register' in 2008. *[Nigel Jones]*

DOXA

Now over 45 years old, *Doxa* (169/1962) has, like many of the tugs featured here, spent more time in Hellenic waters than in British. One of a trio built for Clyde Shipping Co. Ltd. by Ferguson Brothers (Port Glasgow) Ltd., *Flying Mist* was sold to Greek buyers in 1981. Initially named *Poseidon II*, she became *Doxa* in 1986 and has retained the name through a number of subsequent ownerships. Despite a reported sale to breakers in 2005, she was found to be still in full working order at Corfu late in 2006. *[Paul Boot]*

MEGALOCHARI XII

The *Megalochari XII* (156/1967) was built by Richard Dunston Ltd., Hessle as the *Ironsider* for Lawson-Batey Tugs Ltd., Newcastle-upon-Tyne and she faithfully served on the River Tyne for a quarter of a century till sold in summer 1992 to Proodos Naftiki Eteria (managed by Megalochari Hellenic Tugboats), Greece. Like the *Minotavros*, her flying bridge has been removed, to a degree disguising her former identity, though improving her appearance by giving a more balanced profile. Her Greek owner initially repainted her hull from black to white, but at some point red paint has been favoured, as seen on 18th June 2007 when she was approaching the entrance to the Great Harbour, Piraeus after assisting the departure of veteran steam turbine-powered cruise liner *Aegean Two* (12,609/1957). *[Nigel Jones]*

THIELLA

The *Thiella* (173/1962) is seen on 20th September 2004 at Igoumenitsa, an important ferry port on the west coast of Greece, her permanent station. This tug was completed by R. Dunston (Hessle) Ltd. as *Alnmouth* for France, Fenwick Tyne and Wear Co Ltd., a company which was acquired in 1977 by Lawson Batey Ltd. Both companies had been members of the Tyne Tugs Ltd. organisation. *Alnmouth* was then transferred to the latter company, but managed by Lawson Batey. In 1987 she was sold to her present Greek owner, Thiela Shipping Company, the bipod mast and derrick being subsequently fitted. The rendering of her name is debateable; registers listed her as *Thiela* until 2004 and subsequently as *Thyella*. *[Nigel Jones]*

RILLAND

Not all tugs sold to foreign buyers have moved to warmer climes. *Rilland* (115/1953) was one of four tugs of the Tees Towing Co. Ltd. that only ventured across the North Sea when they joined the fleet of William Muller based at Terneuzen on the Scheldt. *Caedmon Cross* had initially been sold to Alexandra Towing in 1966 and as *Margam* served them at Swansea and Liverpool until bought by Muller four years later. Sold by Mullers at the end of 1989, *Rilland* sank shortly after whilst crossing the Bay of Biscay. She was photographed at Terneuzen in April 1987. *[David Salisbury]*

WAASLAND

The Richard Dunston-built *Marton Cross* (115/1963) was bought by William Muller in 1981 together with the older *Fiery Cross* (192/1957) and was photographed at Terneuzen in July the following year. Transferred to the ownership of Sleepboot Mij. 'Zwitzerland' B.V. three years later, *Waasland* is believed to be still in existence. *[David Salisbury]*

UNITED STATES RESERVE FLEET
Photographs by Marc Piché

Marc Piché has supplied these photographs of ships laid up in the James River, Virginia as part of the United States Reserve Fleet. The first two show that the ships are still moored in time-honoured fashion, alternately by bow and by stern. And yes, there is at least one war standard ship still here, the Liberty *Arthur M. Huddell* (7,240/1943). After carrying pipes for Operation PLUTO in 1944, she was laid up at the James River site, but reactivated as a cable transporter in 1956. She returned to lay up in 1984, and has since been a source of spares for the operating Liberty *John W. Brown*. To starboard of *Arthur M. Huddell* is another veteran, the Victory-type attack transport USS *Gage* which carries the number 168.

Undoubtedly the best-known vessel photographed is the nuclear-powered *Savannah* of 1962, seen under tow at Norfolk, Virginia on 31st May 2007. It was expected that she was to be moved to a permanent lay berth at Baltimore, Maryland in May 2008. Her nuclear fuel was removed about 30 years ago.

Another ship with a nuclear past is the *Sturgis* (above). Built as the Liberty *Charles H. Cugle* (7,221/1945), her hull was enlarged in 1964 and had a nuclear power plant installed. As a floating power plant, she was operated by the US Army Corps of Engineers and provided electrical power to the Panama Canal Zone. She was decommissioned and laid up in the James River in 1976. Clearly, given the controversy over scrapping conventional vessels containing asbestos, disposing of this vessel is going to be a difficult exercise.

Two former Lykes Lines ships feature amongst the laid-up ships. *Cape Charles* (middle) was *Charlotte Lykes* (9,296/1963) until 1986, a product of Bethlehem Steel Co. Inc. Shipbuilding Division at Sparrows Point, Maryland. It was reported that she was to be sold for breaking up in August 2007. Until 1985, *Cape Canso* (bottom) was *Aimee Lykes* (9,397/1963), built by Avondale Shipyard Inc. at Avondale, Louisiana.

Renamed in 1977 simply by deleting the 'Mormac' element of their names are the former Moore-McCormack freighters *Lake* (left) and *Pride* (above). *Mormaclake* (9,301/1961) and *Mormacpride* (9,252/1960) were both built by the Sun Shipbuilding and Dry Dock Co, Chester, Pennsylvania. In August 2007, *Pride* was due to be sold for breaking up.

Patriot State (11,188/1964) (below) was the former Grace Lines' *Santa Mercedes*, built by Bethlehem Steel at Sparrows Point, Maryland. Her name was changed to *Patriot State* in 1984.

To conclude the selection of Marc's photographs, this is a view of Unit 5a on the James River on 22nd September 2005. Nearest the camera is the United States Navy's destroyer tender *Cape Cod,* completed in 1982.

As well as being a photographer, Robert Moffat Scott was an avid recorder of livery details of ships calling at South Africa in the 1940s and 1950s. His collection was left to the World Ship Society and these samples are illustrated by courtesy of the Society and the Custodian of its Ships Liveries Section, J.L. Loughran. The individual sheets also include type-written descriptions of colours of hull, waterline, superstructure and masts and notes of other distinguishing features.

Top left: Nederlandsche Nieuw Guinee Petroleum Maatschappij, Batavia.

Top right: Navigazione Libera Giuliana, Venice.

Bottom left: Aktiebolaget Helsingfors Steamship Co. Ltd. (Henry Nielsen Aktiebolaget O/Y). Hesingfors, Finland.

The upper flag is that of the company. The lower is that used when vessels are operating a joint service with Northern Chartering O/Y, designated the Finnish-Africa-Australia Line.

Bottom right: Claymore Shipping Company, London. There is a note on the sheet that the blue is very dark and from a distance is indistinguishable from black.

PHOTOGRAPHER IN FOCUS

ROBERT MOFFAT SCOTT

Peter Newall

The latter part of the 1940s was probably one of the most interesting periods in the maritime history of South Africa. As the nation struggled to establish its own identity, which also unfortunately ushered in the Nationalist Government in 1948, a number of new South African registered shipping companies were formed. Most of these used old tonnage and folded after a few years. Local Cape Town photographer Robert Moffat Scott not only recorded these companies in his detailed notes, he also photographed many of the ships, no matter how small they were. His unique record of this time makes up this celebration of Robert Moffatt Scott's photographic achievements.

Relatively little is know about Moffat's early life except that in his late teens he joined Union-Castle Line in 1921. He worked in the Union-Castle offices in Mombasa and Beira before returning to Cape Town in 1944. In 1957 he was promoted to head of the baggage and claims department in Cape Town docks. He was also one of the first South Africans to become a fellow of the Institute of Chartered Shipbrokers.

The Union-Castle dock office in Cape Town was situated at A Berth and close to the entrance of Duncan Dock. In those days the Union-Castle mailships arrived from the coast on Monday morning and sailed promptly at 4pm on Friday for Southampton. Moffat was therefore ideally placed to observe the shipping movements from his office window. He did not drive or own a car so came to work on the bus from his home at Sea Point, a coastal suburb not far from the city. If a ship was sailing in the afternoon from the old Victoria Basin, he would catch a bus to Number 7 Quay where he kept a bicycle and a large garden umbrella in a small storeroom. He would then ride to his preferred vantage point at the end of the breakwater. He had a large-format-negative bellows camera, which he would place on the quayside to avoid any camera shake. As a result, his photographs were usually pin sharp. The quayside can be clearly seen in the photograph of *Neptune Star*. He was a large man and, many a time, there was concern that he would fall into the dock.

He would also go out in any weather as recalled by local ship photographer Peter Melliar, who spent much time with Robert in his latter years: 'During severe winter storms, very large powerful waves used to sweep over the inner half of the main breakwater but this did not deter Moffat from going out there. Two systems were used to reach the vantage point at the end of the main breakwater. One, we would both walk along the lower inside ledge of the breakwater, both holding the large garden umbrella. Quite a feat in the strong north westerly gales during winter…large waves cascading over the breakwater would pour down on top of the umbrella instead of sweeping us off should we have been walking on top of the

Robert Moffat Scott

breakwater. Alternatively, we would drive out in my small car during extreme storms where waves of solid water quite often up to a metre high swept over the inner half of the breakwater. Moffat would act as time keeper watching the huge waves to seaward and when there was a lull, calling me to go. Now and then Moffat got it badly wrong - resulting in a huge wave hitting the car half way back. On two occasions we ended up within a foot of going over the edge.'

Despite suffering from angina, Moffat photographed anything he could, even in the most atrocious conditions. Peter once asked why he took a photograph of Port Line's *Port Chalmers* (9,535/1933) sailing into the fog. His reply was that half a *Port Chalmers* was better than no record at all. A few months after Moffat's death one of the reasons for his keen photography became clear when Peter was asked to meet with the Port Captain and the Intelligence Chief of the South African Navy. He was told that Moffat has provided the South African and United States Intelligence Services with ship photographs for a number of years. In Moffat's honour, Peter took over this role from 1959 to 1975.

Moffat was keen to involve others in his passion for ships. Not only did he inspire Peter Melliar to take up ship photography in 1957, he also founded the Cape Town branch of the World Ship Society. A local society news letter 'Flotsam & Jetsam' was first published in June 1953. It was co-edited by Peter Hjul, a professional journalist who became the editor of the excellent 'South African Shipping News and Fishing Review' magazine. Peter was also an opponent of the Apartheid regime and, as an active member of the opposition Liberal Party, fled the country in the 1960s. Despite being poorly printed, these early issues of 'Flotsam & Jetsam' contain useful information on the local shipping scene. Moffat was a stickler for detail and was very interested in flags and funnels. He assisted South African ship owners with the designs for their flags and funnels and in the late 1950s Caltex produced a small book on the subject with drawings by Moffat. His flag and funnel records are now held by the World Ship Society.

At the end of August 1959, despite feeling unwell, Moffat rushed to the seaward side of A Berth to join Peter Melliar in catching the sailing of the Dutch C-3 freighter *Riouw* (10,200/1942). This turned out to be the last ship he photographed. The following day, Tuesday 1st September, he excused himself from a meeting as he could see a Japanese trawler leaving her berth. He ran the length of A Berth past the ship's guard standing at the gangway of the *Pretoria Castle* who knew of Moffat's condition. He never reached the end of A Berth as he collapsed with a heart attack and died. He was only 56.

He was a popular man and his cremation was attended by all the leading people in Cape Town's shipping community. His ashes were taken in a pilot boat and scattered in his beloved Table Bay. His widow sold his library locally and, soon after, I bought three small books, each featuring a bookplate by Laurence Dunn (see right). These were among the first shipping books I owned. Moffat's negatives were purchased by Alex Duncan and these are now in various collections. As for his legacy? Cape Town ship photographers Peter Melliar and Robert Pabst, inspired by Moffat, are still taking photographs in Cape Town, almost 50 years after Moffat's death. 'Flotsam & Jetsam' continues to be published by the Ship Society of South Africa and many ship lovers who have bought Alex Duncan photographs over the years probably have at least one photograph in their collection taken by this larger than life man.

BORDER (right)
N.V. Noord Nederlandse Scheepswerven, Groningen; 1927, 185gt, 101.7 feet. Oil engine 5-cyl. 2SCSA by Petters Ltd., Yeovil
This tiny Dutch-built coaster was among the first ships owned by the Durban-based African Coasters (Pty.) Ltd. which was part owned by the Grindrod family whose business later formed Unicorn Lines and the giant Grindrod transport company. Completed for N.V. Motorschip 'Albion', Rotterdam as *Albion*, in the early 1930s she was sold to the Durban company Albion Shipping Co. (Pty.) Ltd. and placed on the Durban to Port St. Johns coastal trade. The Albion company went into liquidation and she was bought in 1936 by African Coasters and renamed *Border*. After surviving at least two strandings, she was sold to Coastal Steamships, Cape Town in 1946 to replace *Chub* (172/1897) which had been wrecked on a voyage from Port Nolloth to Cape Town. Soon after receiving a new engine *Border* ran aground 50 miles south of Port Nolloth on April Fool's

Day 1947 and was left high and dry. Seen in the background of this May 1946 photo is Elder Dempster Lines's *Calabar* (1,932/1935), which operated on the Takoradi-Lagos-Cape Town coastal service until 1948.

PLETTENBERG (below)
Schiffswerft von Henry Koch, Lübeck; 1904, 1,857gt, 265.7 feet. T. 3-cyl. by J.F. Ahrens, Altona
With her tall funnel and goal post mainmast, the German-built coal burner *Plettenberg* was one of the most distinctive vessels in the post-war Southern African

coastal trade. Completed in 1904 as *Helen Heidmann* for the Hamburg firm H.W. Heidmann, she had nine different owners and eight name changes by the time she was seized as a war prize by the South African Government in December 1941. Thai-owned and named *Visut Kasatri Nawa*, she was taken over by the South African Railways and Harbours Administration and renamed *Plettenberg*. She carried coal from Durban to the Congo River and Point Noire. However, unsuited to this trade because her slow speed inhibited her upstream progress, she was sold in 1947 to African Coasters for use on the Durban to Cape Town route. On 21st October 1948 she sailed from East London for Durban and, about 70 miles to the north east of the port, she hit an obstruction. Taking in water, it was decided that she would return to East London. The local harbour tug *E.S. Styetler* was despatched to assist and not long after she arrived, *Plettenberg* started to sink. A total of 28 crew members, two passengers and the ship's cat were rescued. Unfortunately, two African crew members were lost during this dramatic rescue.

D'ROM AFRIKA
Moss Værft & Dokk, Moss; 1930, 250gt, 116 feet.
T. 3-cyl. by Moss Værft & Dokk, Moss
During the Second World War many of the whale catchers stationed in South African waters were requisitioned for war duties. A number belonged to the Union Whaling Company of Durban and had *Uni* names followed by a Roman numeral. *Uni II* was commissioned in March 1941 as the minesweeper *Nigel*. She was built in 1930 for a Danish whaling firm as *Tas II* and was bought by Union Whaling in 1937. After her war service she was decommissioned in January 1945 and offered for sale. She was bought at auction in May 1946 by the Palestine Afrika Fisheries company of Cape Town and renamed *D'rom Afrika*. Robert photographed her unusual funnel design (left), which consisted of a springbok's head in a Star of David. The remainder of her career was quite remarkable as she became part of the clandestine Palyam (Israel Marine Corps) and was used extensively in the Israeli war of independence. After the formation of the Israel Defence Force in May 1948 she became a naval training ship. In 1960 she was sold to a Greek company and renamed *Olga S*. She was deleted from 'Lloyd's Register' in 1979 because of lack of up-to-date information.

FYND (below)
A/S Porsgrunds M/V, Porsgrunn; 1911, 165gt, 104 feet.
T. 3-cyl. by G.T. Grey, South Shields
Seen here in October 1946 being painted after her reconstruction on the patent slipway in Cape Town's Alfred Basin, is another former whale catcher. As the Norwegian *Tonreau*, she was one of the first whale catchers employed on the South African coast. In 1930 she was sold to the well-known Cape Town fishing firm Irvine and Johnson. Converted into a line fishing vessel, she was renamed *Fynd*. After the war she was laid up. Stripped of her mast, funnel, engines and boiler, she was awaiting a scuttling crew when a local businessman bought the hulk for £50. Her new Cape Town owners, Namaqua Shipping Co. (Pty.) Ltd., planned to transform her for the coastal trade between Cape Town and South West Africa. The hull was virtually rebuilt whilst her engines came from another ex-Norwegian whaler, *Frey* (129/1908). In December 1946 she assisted in the salvage operation to remove cargo from Ellerman Lines' *City of Lincoln* (8,039/1938) which had grounded off Quion Point, about 100 miles east of Cape Town. On 10th December *Fynd* attempted to pull the salvage vessel *Swona* (1925/313) free after she ran aground on Quion Point. Unfortunately a rope wrapped around *Fynd*'s propeller and she too was driven ashore. Interestingly, *Swona* had once been a whale catcher in the Christian Salvesen fleet.

T.S. MCEWEN (above)
Bow, McLachlan and Co. Ltd., Paisley;
1925, 793gt, 160 feet.
T. 6-cyl. by Bow, McLachlan and Co.
Ltd., Paisley
City of Lincoln was eventually refloated
in one of the most remarkable salvage
operations ever mounted on the coast
of South Africa. Unfortunately, whilst
sealing all the open spaces to make
the ship watertight for refloating, the
Dutch salvage expert Captain Derek
van Delden was killed when one of the
hatches blew open. Using a number of
coasters, including *Fynd* and *Swona*,
Captain Delden had successfully
offloaded, in difficult circumstances,
tractors, cars, electrical goods, toys

and many other items of cargo. *City of
Lincoln* was eventually refloated, using
pumped air, in March 1947 and towed
stern first into Cape Town's Duncan
Dock by the powerful South African
Railways and Harbours's steam tug *T.S.
McEwen*. The Ellerman cargo liner had
suffered too much damage and she was
broken up locally. Here *T.S. McEwen*,
known locally as 'smoky Sue', is shown
in 1950 towing the remains of the ship
for scuttling in Table Bay. In 1977, the
tug suffered a similar fate when she was
scuttled off Robben Island.

GRIQUA (below)
Rotterdamsche Droogdok Mij.,
Rotterdam; 1917, 1,480gt, 243.2 feet.

*T. 3-cyl. by Rotterdamsche Droogdok
Mij., Rotterdam*
For a while Thesen's Steamship's
Griqua was the largest coaster on the
South African registry. She started life
as *Lingestroom* and operated on N.V.
Hollandsche Stoomboot Maatschappij of
Amsterdam's cross channel routes. She
was bought in 1937 by South Africa's
oldest shipping line, Thesens Steamship
Co. Ltd., for their joint Durban to Belgian
Congo service with Compagnie Maritime
Belge. Renamed *Griqua* the following
year, she was one of the few coasters
with sufficient power to be capable
of negotiating the River Congo and
reaching the port of Matadi. Despite
a few narrow escapes she operated

throughout the war carrying cargoes of palm oil, coffee and timber. She also had comfortable accommodation for 11 passengers. In 1947 she was sold to the Colonial Steamship Co., Mauritius and renamed *Chamarel*. On 2nd March 1949 whilst at Point des Galets, Reunion with a cargo of cased petroleum, she caught fire and sank after an explosion.

NEPTUNE STAR (right)
Robert Duncan and Co. Ltd., Port Glasgow; 1926, 5,112gt, 404.9 feet. T. 3-cyl. by David Rowan and Co. Ltd., Glasgow

In the 1930s the only deep-sea South African-flagged ships were two whale factory ships and the state-owned cargo steamers managed by the South African Railways and Harbours Administration. The SAR fleet was founded at the end of the First World War and initially owned three ex-German war prize vessels. These were replaced by three purpose-built, 5,000gt vessels ordered from the Robert Duncan yard on the Clyde: *Aloe* (1925), *Erica* (1926) and *Dalia* (1930). They were designed for a triangular trade between South Africa, India and Australia. Natal coal would be carried from Durban to east Indian ports where Indian products would be loaded for Australian destinations. The ships would then sail round the east and south of Australia picking up flour and general cargo for the Union before loading railway sleepers at Bunbury in Western Australia. These sleepers were made from jarrah wood, which was hard-wearing and unavailable in South Africa. Manned by South Africans, these ships offered a unique

training for South African seafarers. Although she survived the war, *Erica* had been dogged by problems throughout her career including severe damage suffered in a storm off the coast of Australia and was laid up for almost a year being repaired. The cost of her lay-up exceeded her value and she was sold in 1949 to a newly established Durban firm, the Neptune Shipping Company. Renamed *Neptune Star*, she is seen here arriving at Cape Town in November 1950. The following year, after a rough voyage to South America, she was sold to Japanese owners and became *Tenpaizan Maru*. She was broken up in 1963.

NATAL COAST (below)
Dublin Dockyard Co. Ltd., Dublin; 1920, 3,078gt, 331 feet.

T. 3-cyl. by McKie and Baxter, Glasgow *Neptune Star's* replacement was a former Australian coastal steamer. Laid down as *War Cloud*, a C-type First World War standard ship, she was completed in 1920 as *Glenstal* for the Limerick Steamship Co. Ltd. and sold the same year to the Adelaide Steamship Company to become *Aldinga*. She remained in the Adelaide fleet for 31 years and was sold to Neptune Shipping in 1951. Like so many South African ships of this era, she too succumbed to the treacherous southern Africa coast. On 30th April 1955, whilst on a voyage from Matadi to Cape Town with a cargo of timber and palm oil, she ran aground in thick fog 23 miles north of Walvis Bay, South West Africa. Soon after this loss, Neptune Shipping sold its sole remaining ship and ceased trading.

HOMEFORD (above)
Smith's Dock Co. Ltd., Middlesbrough;
1918, 629gt, 175.4 feet.
T. 3-cyl. by North Eastern Marine
Engineering Co. Ltd., Sunderland
In 1946 the well-known British firm
Moller Line, through its Durban-based
South African subsidiary, became
involved with two new South African
shipping companies. One was Arden
Hall Steamship Company of Cape Town
whose first ship was *Homeford*. This
extraordinary-looking ship was one of the
First World War Kil class patrol vessels,
designed with a similar shaped bow and
stern to confuse enemy submarines as
to which direction she was travelling.
Completed for the Admiralty as HMS
Killygordon, she was sold in 1920 to a
Newcastle firm. Converted into a cargo
ship, she was renamed *Homeford*, a
name she was to retain for 26 years. In
1927, she and *Mead,* another former
Kil-class (see 'Record' 8, page 259),
were bought by the newly-formed
Smith's Coasters (Pty.) Ltd., Durban
for the coastal sugar trade. In 1942
she was requisitioned by the Admiralty
and carried war supplies, especially
drummed aviation fuel, to the Red Sea
and diesel for the lighthouse at Cape

Guardafui. Purchased in 1946 by Arden
Hall, she was intended to be used on a
new service between Cape Town and
Walvis Bay. She is shown arriving at
Cape Town in November 1946, prior to
a major refit. On completion of this work
she was renamed *Laeveld*. Mollers
provided funds to buy three more ships,
including *Bokkeveld* (see 'Record' 8,
page 260). However, the operation was
not profitable and the company folded
in 1949. *Laeveld* spent the remainder
of her career in Greek hands and as
Panaghia Tinou she grounded near
Trieste on 8th October 1964 and broke
her back.

ALPHA ORANJE (below)
William Gray and Co. Ltd, West
Hartlepool; 1930, 5,198gt, 425.2 feet.
Q. 4-cyl. by Central Marine Engineering
Works, West Hartlepool
The second company in which Moller
participated was a far more ambitious
enterprise. The Alpha South African
Steamship Co. Ltd. was incorporated
in June 1946 with a registered share
capital of £1million. It was founded by
the Johannesburg-based Alpha Industrial
Exploration Co. Ltd. with the main aim
of carrying coal from its collieries in the

Transvaal to South America. Mollers
bought a shareholding in the company
and became the ship managers. The
first vessel to enter the fleet was *Alpha
Oranje*, seen here on South Arm in Cape
Town's Victoria Basin. She was built
at the height of the Great Depression
as *Clumberhall* for the West Hartlepool
Steam Navigation Co. Ltd. and remained
in the fleet until June 1946 when she
was sold to Goulandris Brothers Ltd.
of London and renamed *Ormos*. She
arrived under this name at Cape Town
in December 1946 for renaming and
repainting in the distinctive Alpha colour
scheme i.e. buff superstructure and
orange funnel with four green bands and
a blue letter A. Three more cargo ships
were purchased in 1947, including two
Liberty ships and the former merchant
escort carrier *Empire Macrae*. All were
given South African river names with
an *Alpha* prefix. A T2 tanker followed in
1948 but by then freight costs for shipping South African coal to Buenos Aires
had halved and the company was soon
wound up. *Alpha Oranje* was transferred
to Moller Line and retained her name
until her sale to Toho Kaiun K.K., Tokyo
in 1951. Renamed *Eiko Maru*, she went
to Japanese breakers in 1961.

GENERAL GEORGE BRINK (above)
*William Gray and Co. Ltd, West Hartle-
pool; 1927, 4,892gt, 405.1 feet.*
*T. 3-cyl. by Central Marine Engineering
Works, West Hartlepool*
Another West Hartlepool-built tramp
arrived on the scene in 1946. The
General George Brink was bought by
the Cape Town-based Union Steamship
Company of South Africa Ltd., which
had been established in 1945 by
a syndicate of South African ex-
servicemen. The ship had been named
after General Brink who commanded
the 1st South African Division during
the Second World War. A typical
long bridge deck-type tramp she was
completed as *Rockpool* and was one of
28 ships built between 1925 and 1930
for the famous company Sir Robert
Ropner and Co. Ltd. which originated in
West Hartlepool. In February 1941 she
ran aground in the Firth of Clyde and
was declared a constructive total loss.
She was later salved by the Ministry
of War Transport and renamed *Empire
Trent*. Under the Union Steamship

banner she was used as coal carrier to
the Middle East. Here she is arriving
at Cape Town in September 1946.
Some of the crew appear to have been
unhappy with their food rations as some
wag has written 'Starvation' on the side
of the aft well. Note also that Robert's
camera has been placed on the ground
for this shot. In 1947 she was sold to
a Panamanian company and renamed
Africana. She too ended her days in
a Japanese scrap yard in 1959. The
Union Steamship Company lasted until
1949 when its shares and three small
coasters were acquired by Thesen's
and given *Coast* names. One of these,
Mashona Coast, is featured in 'Record'
8, page 255.

PRESIDENT KRUGER (below)
*Permanente Metals Corporation
Shipyard No.2, Richmond, California;
1943, 7,194gt, 422 feet.*
*T. 3-cyl. by Joshua Hendy Iron Works,
Sunnydale, California*
After the fall of Greece in 1941,
the Greek shipowner Evanghelos

P. Nomikos registered a privately-
owned shipping company, Southern
Steamships (Pty.) Ltd., in Johannesburg.
In 1948 another Nomikos company
came into being, Northern Steamships
(Pty.) Ltd., also registered in
Johannesburg. Through these
companies, the Nomikos family operated
a number of South African registered
ships, all with *President* names. They
were tramp ships and although they
were initially required to carry a majority
of South African crew, they seldom
operated in South African waters. In
1947 and 1948 three Liberty ships were
purchased. *President Kruger* was the
first to be delivered in October 1947.
She was followed by *President Reitz*,
which was wrecked near Port Elizabeth
in November 1947, two days after
being renamed, and *President Steyn*.
President Kruger was launched as *John
M.Palmer* and although she received a
number of different names throughout
her career, she remained in Nomikos
ownership until she was scrapped at
Kaohsiung in 1968.

AELO (above)
Eriksbergs M.V. A/B., Göteborg; 1934, 2,709gt, 339.3 feet.
Oil engine 6-cyl. 2SCDA by Eriksbergs M.V. A/B., Göteborg
Another well-known Greek shipowner was involved with one of the more successful South African shipping companies of the 1940s. Eugen Eugenides, who founded Home Lines, also formed the Cape Town firm, South Africa Lines Ltd., in 1941. It was established to trade between South African ports, West Africa, Brazil and Europe. After the chartered *Argo* (1,995/1920) was torpedoed on a voyage from Buenos Aires to Cape Town in November 1942 with the loss of 12 crew and six passengers the service was suspended until the end of hostilities. Eugenides had close connections with the Swedish firm Broströms (one of its directors was on the SAL board) and it was probably not surprising that the first ship owned by the new company was the former Broström's Swedish Orient Line cargo ship *Vasaland*. On 30th June 1947 she was handed over in Durban and renamed *Aelo*. Her funnel design was similar to the Broström scheme apart from the colour of the bands and SAL initials. She was also the first South African-flagged motor ship. In 1949 all SAL ships were given names ending in -*land* - another aspect possibly copied from Broström - and *Aelo* became *Kaapland*. In the same year, the SAL schedule replicated the pre-war services between Northern Europe and South Africa of Deutsche Ost-Afrika-Linie. By the mid 1950s Deutsche Ost-Afrika-Linie had a controlling interest in South Africa Lines and the original fleet, including *Kaapland*, was replaced with modern German-built ships. Sold in 1954, she traded under a further four names and was only broken up at Gadani Beach in 1978.

CONSTANTIA (below)
Bethlehem-Fairfield Shipyard Inc., Baltimore; 1945, 7,607gt, 439.1 feet.
Two steam turbines by the Westinghouse Electrical and Manufacturing Company, Pittsburgh, Pennsylvania
The company which became South Africa's premier line was of course Safmarine. The new South African Marine Corporation (Pty.) Ltd. was formed on the 21st June 1946 to operate a fast cargo-passenger service between South Africa and New York. It was initially a joint venture with the New York-based States Marine Corporation and its first managing director was the former chief of RAF Bomber Command, Sir Arthur Harris. In August 1946 the new service started with chartered tonnage and reduced the pre-war crossing time by more than a week. Three Victory ships were purchased from the US Maritime Commission and the first to arrive in Cape Town was the former *New Bern Victory*, now renamed *Constantia*, on 22nd August 1947. She was followed later that year by her new consorts *Morgenster* and *Vergelegen*. The names chosen were old Cape Dutch wine estates. *Constantia* is shown here leaving Cape Town on her first voyage along the South African coast to Durban. This trio also had superior air-conditioned accommodation for 12 passengers. Renamed *South African Vanguard* in 1961 and *S.A. Vanguard* in 1966, she was sold to a Panamanian-registered company in 1969. As *Isabena* she capsized in July 1972 near Karachi whilst loading grain from another ship with the loss of five of her crew.

PUTTING THE RECORD STRAIGHT

Letters, additions, amendments and photographs relating to features in any issues of 'Record' are welcomed. Communications by e-mail are quite acceptable, but senders are asked to include their postal address. Letters may be lightly edited.

The editors would deem it a great kindness if readers submitting letters for this column would as far as possible follow our current editorial style, and in particular put ships' names into upper and lower case italics and not capitals.

Department of Correction

Page 74 of 'Record 38' states for British and Continental Steamship Co. Ltd. ship number 22 *Tadorna* that the T. 3-cyl. engine was built by the shipyard. This is not correct as Burntisland never made any engines. It was built by D. and W. Henderson and Co. Ltd., Glasgow and the size of the engine was 21 x 36 x 59 x 39 inches. It would have been fitted by the yard.
JOHN IVES, 2 Hawthorn Bank, Carnock, Dunfermline, Fife KY12 9JS
Bob Todd has pointed out that the sale of Gemma, ex-Merganser, *on page 77 of 'Record' 38 took place in 1970 not 1974. Ed.*

Knowing what sticklers you and Malcolm Cooper are for accuracy, you may wish to correct names on page 190 of 'Record' 39.

The second corvette was HMCS *Edmundston*. Her pennant number K 106 is just visible in a photograph on the next page. The third tug was surely the *Tatnuck* not *Tantunk*, even though both sound equally unlikely.
JOHN BARTLETT, 6 Cottenham Park Road, London SW20 0RZ

Melmay causing confusion

A comparison with a picture in my collection does not support the notion that the ship on page 184 of 'Record' 39 is the *Melmay* which became *Lagosian*. A similar silhouette, for sure, but my picture shows the ship when virtually new entering Vancouver harbour possibly on her first voyage into Vancouver. (I was originally under the impression that she never made it to Vancouver before the financial problems faced by her first owner overtook the ownership, but I was wrong as the picture proves.)

The ship depicted in 'Record' 39 may be an earlier Dollar ship, but she has four masts and most noticeable is the bridge, a sketchy affair over a tiny wheelhouse, typical of the period up to about the end of the 19th century. The *Melmay* had a proper enclosed wheelhouse and bridge wing houses and crosstrees typical of the 1930s on her three masts. Also the amidships accommodation was extended out to the full width of the ship. The Robert Dollar Line of San Francisco sported the well-known black funnel with the white dollar sign, whereas the Chief Line, Melville Dollar's Canadian-based Canadian American Shipping Company, relied on the simple black funnel depicted in the photo.
SYD HEAL, 8415 Granville Street, Box 46, Vancouver, British Columbia, Canada V6P 4Z9

Syd Heal's letter on the origins of the *Melmay* provides a useful perspective on an unusual vessel. However, she was hardly the first new building for the Dollar family. Prior to the First World War they had ships built for them by A. Rodger and Co. which sailed under British flag: *Bessie Dollar* (4,329/1905), *Hazel Dollar* (4,304/1905), and *Robert*

Despite a note on the back claiming that it represented *Melmay*, the photograph reproduced on page 194 of 'Record' 39 was clearly not the ship that later became *Lagosian*. The ship depicted has been the subject of intensive research by William Schell and Ian Farquhar who, with the help of digital enhancement of the image, have concluded quite convincingly that it is the *Chelston* (3,687/1904). This ship, which 'Lloyd's

Register' describes as having four masts and three islands, was built by A. Rodger and Co., Glasgow for T.L. Duff and Co. Both Duff's funnel (buff with black top and narrow blue band) and house flag (11 alternating red and white horizontal stripes with a St Andrews cross in the upper canton of the hoist) match those in the photograph, and enlarging the image shows that *Chelston* fits with what can be read of her name on the bow. *Chelston* was

owned by Duff throughout her life, which ended when she was wrecked on St Paul's Island in the Gulf of St. Lawrence on 13th September 1919. Duff also owned the *Melmay*, so it is likely that whoever wrote that name on the back had gone some way towards identifying the ship from her markings and layout.

The editors are certain that the ship depicted in the photo reproduced here is *Melmay*. [Basil Feilden/J. and M. Clarkson]

Dollar (5,356/1911), as well as other new buildings under the US flag. *Bessie Dollar* and *Hazel Dollar* are shown in 'Lloyd's Register' as four-masted ships and a late photo of one of them shows a layout very similar to that of the *Melmay*.

Furthermore, *Melmay* was not put in the management of T.L. Duff and Co. by creditors. It would appear they were managers from the start. I have a 1930 'Lloyd's Register' with the new entries pasted in the blank pages and the entry for the *Melmay* immediately following delivery shows Duff as managers.
WILLIAM SCHELL, 334 South Franklin Street, Holbrook, MA 02343, USA

Trials in ballast
On page 182 of 'Record' 39 a comment was made that *Scottish Hawk* is in fully loaded condition [this referred to a photograph on page 339 of 'Clan Line: Illustrated Fleet List': ed]. This is normal when tankers are on trials, as they can be ballasted down to almost their load draught, thereby giving a genuine speed at that draught, as opposed to a dry cargo ship that cannot be ballasted to anything like her load draught on trials. The advantage is that there is no need in the case of tankers to extrapolate the trial results to the full loaded condition, which has to be corrected in the case of dry cargo vessels. As an example, the British India tanker *Queda* ran trials in 1959 at a draught of 29 feet 6 inches, her loaded draught being 30 feet 2 inches; whereas in the same year *Bulimba*, a British India dry cargo ship, ran trials at a draught of 14 feet 6 inches, her loaded draught being 25 feet 1 inch.
TONY SMYTHE, 35 Avondale Road, Rayleigh, Essex SS6 8NJ

Accumulated additions
'Record' 24
I have been able to identify two of the unnamed craft in my article on Garston beginning on page 241 of 'Record' 24, thanks to Craig Carter's article on Garston's dredging fleet in 'Record' 31.

On page 243 the steam hopper on the extreme left of the photo is in fact the steam grab hopper dredger *North Western* of 1908. This vessel is also shown in the photo on page 249 berthed on the south quay of the North Dock. There is an excellent photo of her on page 175 of 'Record' 31.

Incidentally, the dock in which *North Western* and *New Pioneer* are berthed is the North Dock not the Old Dock. The Old Dock is in the foreground of the photo on page 249.
'Record' 26
Page 95: sale of *Inniscroone* in 1939 was to Wadsworth <u>Lighterage</u> and Coaling Co. Ltd. (*not* Wadsworth <u>Lightering</u> and Coaling Co. Ltd.)
'Record' 27
Page 140: the middle photo of *Mary Kingsley* has to have been taken on the Mersey at some time prior to May 1951 for lying alongside her is the City of Liverpool (Port Health Authority) motor tender *Moyles* of 1928, which is featured on pages 105,106 and 108 of 'Record' 26 (Stephen Carter's excellent article on Harry Rose's *Wendy Ann* tugs).
'Record' 28
Page 257: lower right illustration - *Capitan Segarra* is not approaching a port for she is not under way but at anchor as demonstrated by the black ball hoisted forward over the forecastle.
'Record' 31
Garston's Dredging Fleet - page 175 - a fascinating article - but sadly no mention is made of the following craft that served with this fleet:

motor hopper barge *Aigburth* of 1963 (registered at Liverpool)
trailing suction dredger *Afan* of 1961 (registered at Cardiff)
trailing suction dredger *Baglan* of 1966
motor grab hopper dredger *Aberavon* of 1969
trailing suction dredger *UKD Dolphin* of 1984.

Admittedly, the last four were usually on loan from South Wales ports of British Transport Docks/ABP but nevertheless they spent some considerable time actually based at Garston, and were (or are in the case of *UKD Dolphin*) familiar sights on the Mersey.

Aigburth working at Milford Haven in September 1970. *[J. and M. Clarkson]*

'Record' 32

Page 218: Colin Menzies asks for any information on S. Catsell and Co. According to the 'Greek Shipping Directory' of 1965 S. Catsell and Co. Ltd. were domiciled at 6 Bevis Marks, London EC3, the directors being S. Catsell and B.R. Catsell. They were London representatives for two Greek vessels owned by Marcasa Compania Naviera S.A., Panama:

> *St. Anthony* (5,349/1940) ex *Winkleigh* 1960 of W.J. Tatem
>
> *St. Nicholas* (7,165/1942) ex *Avisvale* 1961 of Aviation and Shipping Co. Ltd.

I.G. Stewart's 'British Tramps' on page 269 shows the firm being established in 1943 and operating some five vessels under the auspices of the Kenfig Steamship Co. Ltd. up until 1958 and the Noemijulia Steamship Co. Ltd. up to 1948 (both presumably on behalf of Greek beneficial owners.).

The aforementioned edition of the 'Greek Shipping Directory' has the Kenfig Steamship Co. Ltd. at 63/65 Crutched Friars, London EC3 acting as London representatives for the two ships listed above under S. Catsell plus the following Greek vessels:

> *Noemi* (7,070/1942) ex *Sabrina* 1961, ex *Ovingdean Grange* 1959, ex *Empire Buckler* 1946.
>
> *St. Antonio* (7,051/1943) ex *Olga Minacoulis* 1964, ex *Lord Gladstone* 1958, ex *Empire Mortimer* 1947.

'Record' 32 page 260; 'Record' 33 page 53; and 'Record' 35 page 146

With reference to the *Zealandia* of 1875 it may be of interest that whilst I was navigating from Liverpool to Preston in September 1999 and as I approached Southport just as the tide was beginning to flood, I observed through the haze and with the aid of binoculars a structure protruding from the surface. However, by the time I reached this position the tide had flooded sufficiently to cover the evidence and I began to wonder if it had been an illusion.

However, on a repeat voyage in September 2003, on approaching the same position at a similar state of the tide, there was a yellow conical buoy in the position where I had observed the protrusion in 1999. My curiosity was further aroused when reaching the buoy to find that it had *Zealandia* written on it in black letters. 'Records' 33 and 35 of course solved the mystery. I was also relieved that I had not been half an hour later in 1999 - otherwise, I might well have made unexpected contact with the remains!

The buoy and (at low water) the wreckage of *Zealandia* are still visible from the shore at Ainsdale. A photo of the wreckage in September 2000 (before the arrival of the buoy) can be seen at www.martyngriff.co.uk.

'Record' 34

Pages 113-114: Challis, Stern and Co. Ltd., London was still going strong in the 1970s - or at least its name was - for they were the purveyors of the famous 'Four Bells Rum' to be found in the bond locker (and elsewhere!) of many a good British merchant ship.

NIGEL BOWKER, 9 Boulton Green Close, Spital, Bebington, Wirral, Cheshire

Photinia lays cables

In 'Record' 37 there was a photo of Stag Line's bulker *Photinia* at Manchester, and a brief mention that she had been used as a cable layer between 1962 and 1965. She became well known in New Zealand during that period as she laid three British Insulated Callender's Cables Ltd. (BICC) electric power cables across Cook Strait between Oteranga Bay (North Island) and Fighting Bay (South Island).

For use in Cook Strait her forward hold was converted to house a cable engine and equipment for a Voith-Schneider bow propulsion unit. The second hold was used to store and handle the numerous additional items required. Her next three holds were adapted to carry the cables, whilst her after hold provided accommodation for the 40-man cable crew. Various deck fittings were installed, such as a roller-train along one side to transport the cable to the bow, a cable-laying control, large sheaves on the forecastle head and a bell-mouth over the bow. The equipment was installed early in 1962 and sea trials were carried out in Scottish waters later that year, after which the cable-laying equipment was

Photinia, complete with bow sheaves, in the Cook Strait on 3rd May 1977. *[J. and M. Clarkson collection]*

removed and she resumed normal trading whilst the cables were being manufactured. In February 1964 she arrived at South Shields for the cable-laying equipment to be re-installed and more trials and practice runs were repeated in 1964. She was then loaded with three 41-kilometre lengths of 5-inch cable directly from the BICC cable factory at Trafford Park near Manchester. She sailed from Manchester in August 1964 for New Zealand.

The power cables were laid across Cook Strait between November and December 1964. After testing, one cable required some repair work, and this was not completed until May 1965, after many delays caused by bad weather in Cook Strait. *Photinia* then returned to UK and loaded more cable at Trafford Park, and I observed her sailing outbound from the Ship Canal on 7th August 1965. She laid this cable between Trinidad and Tobago in September 1965, after which her cable-laying equipment was removed and placed into storage on the Tyne and she returned to normal trading.

Many years later, a fault developed in one of the cables, and *Photinia* was again fitted with the cable-laying equipment and sailed for New Zealand to carry out the repair work, arriving in Wellington in May 1977 and taking about a month to complete the work, again returning to the Tyne to land her special equipment. Less than a year after her final visit to New Zealand waters, she was driven aground in a storm in the Great Lakes, was badly damaged and was later scrapped locally.
CAPTAIN MICHAEL PRYCE, 65 Amesbury Drive, Churton Park, Wellington 6037, New Zealand

Empire May-class
The letter from Ian Ramsay in 'Record' 38 left me more than a little puzzled as it did not accord with my understanding of the story of the *Empire May-* class.

So I consulted 'Lloyd's Register' and found that his offerings were half right. According to the register the *Loch Broom* was indeed re-engined with a British Polar at Ardrossan, and indeed had been built by Scotts of Bowling. But Lloyd's Register shows she was built as the *Empire Maysong*, not *Empire Mayring*.

The *Loch Frisa* was a more exotic creature. Built in 1946 as the *Ottawa Maycliff* by Morton Engineering and Dry Dock Company of Quebec, to the same dimensions as the other *Empire May-* vessels, this class appears to have been spread fairly widely for their construction. (Interesting question: how many were built in total?). Ian's description then aligns with the 'Lloyd's Register' record.

And the *Empire Mayring*? 'Lloyd's Register's' record is corroborated by the builder's records held by Eric Hammal, naval architect for Cochranes of Selby for their final 30 years. He kept a substantial archive including the yard's building lists. These show the *Empire Mayring* as Cochranes' yard number 1305, delivered from Selby in January 1946. Yard number 1306, incidentally, was the *Empire Mayrover*, delivered in May 1946. The placing of *Empire Mayring's* management with W.N. Lindsay Ltd. then fits, as do the photos of *Empire Mayring* ('Record' 36) on trials against a backdrop of the Hull waterfront, and her eventual sale to the Far East ('Record' 35).
DOUGLAS J. LINDSAY, 3 Rectory Court, Old Banwell Road, Locking, Weston-super-Mare BS24 8BS
Ian Ramsay corrected his mistake in 'Record' 39. Ed.

Man who dropped the Stülcken
I was especially taken by A.D. Frost's point (page 182 of 'Record' 39) about Clan Line's avoidance of the Stülcken derrick. As he suspects, the royalty story was one of those myths that deserve the fate that Andrew Bell recommends in his letter elsewhere in the issue. I would guess, however, that Stülcken would have enjoyed a handsome licensing fee and I think that many of these derricks had to be actually installed and tested at their Hamburg yard.

Some of your readers might have ideas on the cost of such a derrick and others might know just how much freight a heavy-lift was worth in certain trades but I think that many of us would recall the use of the 'jumbo' as one of the minor episodes in any voyage. That being so, maybe Clan Line (and many other companies) thought that the initial investment was unlikely to be repaid that easily. The Stülcken derrick was of course much quicker to break out and house than a conventional heavy derrick and it could be used at two hatches but it needed extra knowledge from those using it. Believe me, when you had to pull the cargo blocks through that Y-fork on the top of the earlier models, you had to know what you were doing.

Maybe I am biased in that judgement but I do know that a Stülcken derrick figured in one of the lowest points of my seagoing career. I was on T. and J. Harrison's *Trader* and we had used the Stülcken extensively in Aberdeen unloading oilfield equipment in February 1975. It was getting dark and our berth was wanted so there was the usual sailing panic. I had a 'run' crowd who were making a right hash of trying to house two of the smaller derricks into the mast clamps alongside the Stülcken. To be fair to them, however, the ship's unavoidably large stern trim did not help. So I agreed to these derricks being stood off for the passage round to the Mersey. Incidentally, we had no crutching arrangements for us to carry these derricks horizontally (the illustration of Shaw Savill's *Zealandic* on page 178 shows how). We sailed and I was blissfully unaware that the bosun had tightened up the cargo runners on these two small derricks as an added precaution. This meant that the winch barrels of the two Stülcken spans were 'out of gear' and so the derrick was only secured by the winch drum brakes and the mast clamps.

Early the next morning we went into the Pentland Firth and began dipping into the Atlantic swell. The North Sea pilot and myself were enjoying a cup of coffee together on the bridge when all hell broke loose. The Stülcken had burst its bonds and was heading downwards. Not very fast: there are a lot of sheaves for the wires to negotiate, but a sobering firework display of sparks until the derrick gently came to rest on the hatch with its head blocks hanging drunkenly over the bulwark. To cut the story short, that is how we came in through the Langton entrance and, whilst I escaped the sack, I put in many, many hours of unpaid overtime being required to attend the repair works. Amazingly, there was virtually no damage, even to the heel bearings and trunnion, just the general shame of being the man who dropped the jumbo overside. So, yes, no Stülckens here, thanks!
JOHN GOBLE, 55 Shanklin Road, Southampton SO15 7RG

Sea water in the phosphorus
The letter from David Burrell on page 185 of 'Record' 39 reminds me of a similar problem when I worked for Albright

Harrison's *Trader* with Stülcken secured. *[FotoFlite/J. and M. Clarkson collection]*

and Wilson. In the early 1950s we built a new phosphorus plant alongside Portishead Dock. The technology was the same as used in our earlier plants at Oldbury and Widnes and we relied on imported Florida phosphate rock as our main raw material. A problem arose very quickly as unexpected holes appeared in the stainless steel parts of the plant. After blaming several other factors, we eventually decided that the problem was hydrogen chloride corroding the steel. Florida rock was used because it was particularly low in chloride and had not caused this problem in our other plants. We had tested the rock when it arrived and found it in spec. It was only when we got down into the bottom of the holds and tested the material there that we discovered chloride contamination.

The problem was that old tramps which were used to ship the rock had leaked and let small amounts of sea water into the cargo, hence the chloride levels and the problem. After the rejection of one or two cargoes there was an improvement but rogue lots were difficult to detect before a significant part of the load was discharged.

As a consequence we had a ship built specially for our exclusive use. This ship *Arthur Albright* (6,646/1960) had, according to eyewitnesses, the distinction of being launched bearing three names, *Arthur Albright*, *Arthur Allbright* and *Arthur Allright*. She sailed between Portishead and Florida for a number of years.
TONY SMITH, 24 Balmoral Road, Kingsdown, near Deal, Kent CT14 8DB

Arthur Albright. [Fotoship/J. and M. Clarkson collection]

Perthshire still with yards on her foremast. She lost these during her long and rather involved naval career. *[Ian J. Farquhar collection]*

Buteshire (2) arriving at Avonmouth with her more substantial forward 'funnel'. *[Ian J. Farquhar collection]*

SCOTTISH SHIRE LINE: Part 2

Ian J. Farquhar

By the early 1890s the entire focus of Turnbull, Martin was directed at the New Zealand frozen meat trade with London, as well as securing what general cargo was available at the ports at which the ships loaded the meat. A further three, slightly larger, steamers were completed with the *Buteshire* and *Perthshire* entering service in 1893, followed by the *Banffshire* in 1894. They had a refrigerated capacity for 100,000 carcases of mutton, twice that of the previous trio. The seven ships enabled a monthly service to be maintained, although Turnbull, Martin was still reliant on the ships being chartered to one of the other Conference lines on the outward voyage to Australia or New Zealand. Shaw, Savill and Albion even chartered Shire vessels when it suited, if only to prevent other lines becoming familiar with the New Zealand trade. A typical voyage in the 1890s saw the vessels loading out from London to Adelaide, Melbourne and Sydney to discharge, then loading frozen cargo at Townsville or Rockhampton, back to Newcastle or Sydney for coal bunkers before heading across the Tasman to load the majority of the northbound cargo in New Zealand. The four early ships, including *Elderslie*, were sold between 1897 and 1899 being replaced by newer, larger editions of *Morayshire, Fifeshire* and *Banffshire*. The three new vessels had increased refrigerated capacity.

Marine mishaps

The company was not immune from maritime incidents. On 2nd October 1894 the *Buteshire* was picked up in the Indian Ocean in position 40.18 south by 66.10 east by the *Strathord* (4,040/1894). She had lost her propeller and was towed to

Mauritius, arriving on 14th October. The same vessel lost two of her propeller blades on 10th March 1896 while on passage from New Zealand to London and had to slowly make her way back the 1,671 miles to Auckland. In March 1897, while proceeding from London to Australia along the southern ocean, *Nairnshire* collided with an iceberg, causing a leak in her forepeak. Three months later *Morayshire*, while coasting from Sydney to Bowen, broke her tail shaft and damaged her stern tube. She was picked up by the China Navigation Company's steamer *Chingtu* (2,268/1886) and towed to Keppel Bay, where the *Nairnshire* took over the tow to Brisbane. On 19th October 1898 *Buteshire* had a serious fire while lying alongside in Sydney.

On 28th August 1896 *Fifeshire*, on passage from Queensland to Bluff in New Zealand, was lucky to see distress signals from the wooden US sailing ship *Patrician* (1,254/1879) which was on a course from Newcastle, New South Wales to Lyttelton with 1,800 tons of coal. The *Patrician* had encountered very rough weather, with several sails carried away, all the boats stove in and the pumps unable to cope with the inflow of water. *Fifeshire* lost the first boat put out to go and rescue the crew of *Patrician* and the master, Captain Wilson, refused to allow his chief officer to try and swim to the sinking vessel with a line. It was finally agreed to launch the pinnace and Captain E.R. Sterling and his crew were finally taken aboard the *Fifeshire*. The *Patrician* was abandoned in sinking condition in position 39.8 south by 158.11 east. As a sequel to the rescue, George Ross, first officer of the *Fifeshire*, was awarded Lloyd's Silver Medal for saving life at sea, and G.

Morayshire (2) of 1898. She served as a troopship during the Boer War, and this photograph is presumed to have been taken on 2nd April 1901 as she sailed from Southampton for Capetown with 18 officers and 1,076 men. *[Newall Dunn collection]*

An artist's impression of the *Talune* towing the *Perthshire*. *[Ian J. Farquhar collection]*

Mowatt, bosun, and J.L. Martin, a quartermaster, both received Lloyd's Bronze Medals.

The most serious incident related to the *Perthshire*. She had sailed from Sydney for Bluff in southern New Zealand in ballast on 26th April 1899 and on the 28th she broke her tail shaft about 391 miles south east from Sydney in position 38.37 south by 156.48 east. Sails were rigged but the vessel would not steer even with every stitch of canvas set and she kept drifting north east so that by 28th May she had drifted 930 miles. The engineers had initially abandoned any idea of temporary repairs but desperation was apparent when there were no responses to the rockets and distress signals sent, even though *Perthshire* was close to a main steamer track. The schooner *Whangaroa* (143/1893) had sighted her on 13th May, and then the barque *Northern Chief* (287/1886) was spoken to on 25th May. It was finally decided to break away the stern tube and endeavour to couple the broken shaft. Two hundred small holes were drilled into the tube to make it split. At the same time chains were passed around the propeller on the outside of the vessel. This task was extremely difficult and, after two experiences of the gear carrying away, the propeller and part of the tail shaft, weighing nearly 13 tons, were held in position and the brass tubing cut away. The space in which the men had to work was extremely small and the whole operation involved arduous and dangerous work. A portion of the stern tube was cut back in order to fix on the coupling and in some instances this had to be accomplished by means of wedges eight feet in length, worked from above the tubing. As soon as the shaft was ready, the coupling, in three parts (each weighing half a ton) was lowered with great care and fitted to the broken end of the shaft. This work took three full days. On 7th June the ship *Verajean* (1,941/1891) was sighted and it was not until 11th June, after fourteen days of extremely hard work which had lasted around the clock, that the first few turns of the propeller were taken. After six weeks of silence the engines were back in service, the temporary structure worked satisfactorily and the ship made steerage way. At the time she was within 46 miles of the rock-bound coast of Norfolk Island. The following day she steamed 83 miles to the west, in between stoppages to inspect the temporary repair and make adjustments to the couplings where required. The fate of the *Perthshire* had become a

major issue in all the newspapers and conjecture about the vessel was widespread throughout Australia and New Zealand. Ships were requested to deviate from their normal courses to try and locate *Perthshire* and, over one period, nine vessels were searching for her. After *Perthshire* had steamed about 184 miles on her makeshift rig she was sighted by the Union Company steamer *Talune* (2,087/1890) in position 29.03 south by 163.38 east at 03:30 hours on 13th June. The *Talune* was on a regular voyage from Auckland to Sydney and had been asked to take a more northern course to keep a look-out for the missing *Perthshire*. Captain Christopher Spinks of the *Talune* had made a study of ocean currents and, as *Talune* searched to the north of her normal track, she kept firing rockets each hour in the hope that the *Perthshire* might respond. She had actually fired her last rocket when an answering rocket was sent up by the *Perthshire*. She was taken in tow by the *Talune* and, after numerous mishaps with the towing hawser, *Perthshire* was towed 710 miles to Sydney and arrived on 19th June. She finally reached her original destination of Bluff at the end of July 1899. A salvage award of £5,000 was made to the *Talune* and Captain James Wallace and Chief Engineer John Blair of *Perthshire* were each awarded Lloyd's Medal for Meritorious Services. Captain Wallace retired in 1930 as commodore of the Clan Line fleet and he died in 1934. Two years after the *Perthshire* disappearance, Captain Spinks, then in command of the Union Company's *Mokoia* (3,502/1898), used his knowledge of ocean currents to locate the trans-Tasman liner *Monowai* (3,433/1890) which had been drifting south of New Zealand after losing two propeller blades on 17th October 1901, but fortunately she was located four days later.

The Shire fleet had another spate of mishaps in the early years of the twentieth century including a number of minor fires. They started with the *Buteshire* when she put into Fremantle in May 1901 with the cargo on fire, causing considerable damage. In January 1905 the same vessel, on passage from New York to Australia, diverted to Cape Town to quench a fire which seriously damaged the ship and cargo. *Buteshire* was in the news three years later when she stranded in the Thames on 27th December 1908 at the end of a voyage from Argentina to London. She was hauled off with the assistance of several tugs on the following day, resulting in a

£7,275 salvage award. On 1st August 1909 *Buteshire* was in collision with the *Relillio* (2,420/1909) five miles north west of Ushant in heavy fog as she was proceeding from London to Buenos Aires. *Buteshire* was hit abaft the bridge, indenting several plates. The *Perthshire* was back in the news in June 1906 when she arrived at Las Palmas with the cargo in number 4 hold on fire. A quantity of wool and tow was jettisoned and she was able to continue her voyage, arriving in London on 11th June. The *Nairnshire* had a fire at Auckland on 11th December 1909 but it was quickly extinguished. Two years later in September 1911 she put into Montevideo with her crank shaft broken. *Morayshire* was in collision with the collier *Axwell* (1,442/1909) off Gravesend on 31st January 1911 at the end of a voyage from Sydney to London. She suffered bow damage. On 2nd January 1910 the *Ayrshire* collided with the Ellerman steamer *Arcadian* (2,855/1891) in thick fog near Tuskar Rock, in St. George's Channel, six miles off the coast of Wexford, Ireland. *Ayrshire* was on passage from Manchester to Durban. She immediately started to take in water and was towed to Holyhead and beached. The *Arcadian* foundered with the loss of 12 lives. On 2nd July 1914, in position 4.41 north by 12.35 west, while *Ayrshire* was proceeding from Liverpool to Australia, fire was discovered in number 3 hold and, although the ship did everything to fight the fire, it was not extinguished until *Ayrshire* reached Cape Town on 13th July and shore appliances dealt with it. There was 23 feet of water in number 3 hold and considerable damage to the cargo throughout the ship requiring all of it to be discharged in Cape Town.

Caird, Hughes and the Cayzers

Turnbull's partner, Edward Martin, died on 6th February 1900, at the age of 51, but management of the line had been steadily assumed by James Caird, who had married Edward Martin's sister and had started in the London office in 1889. From 1899 Caird's name appears in official registration documents as the manager of the steamers in place of Edward Martin, and by 1903 he was the sole remaining partner. However, over the following years, the greatest influence on the course of the

company came from outside in the form of Allan Hughes, a remarkable leader who was a major influence in Australian and New Zealand liner shipping from 1903 to 1928. Hughes formed the Meteor Steam Navigation Company in London in 1892, renaming it the King Steam Navigation Company in 1894 and then Federal Steam Navigation Company from 1895. Hughes' brokerage firm of Allport and Hughes combined with J. Gavin Birt and John Potter and Company to form the partnership of Birt, Potter and Hughes in 1895 and three years later it became a limited liability company. Hughes gained a majority interest in this company in 1903. He saw a great potential for the Federal Steam Navigation Company in developing shipping services from Australia and New Zealand. He was involved with a service from New Zealand to South Africa in 1902 and in 1902 and 1903 he began buying New Zealand meat to sell in Britain and sent his Federal Line vessels to load it. For some years exporters in the west of England and Scotland had been pushing New Zealand Shipping and Shaw, Savill and Albion to provide them with a direct service to New Zealand from west coast ports. Their calls were largely ignored and, when the New Zealand Government called for tenders for such a service at the end of 1903, Hughes successively combined his Federal Line with the two smaller companies in the trade - Houlder Brothers and Turnbull, Martin - to form the Federal-Houlder-Shire Line to win the tender. He now had a legitimate protection for a trade share through this contract and Federal-Houlder-Shire aggressively commenced a southbound service from May 1904 and a direct west coast return service from New Zealand was inaugurated in December 1905. When the Federal-Houlder-Shire vessels could not secure full cargoes for the west coast they began calling at London as well. This provoked a full rate war and this was not finally resolved until October 1906 when the three lines agreed to share the New Zealand trade under a seven-year pooling agreement, although the arrangement excluded Tyser and Company.

Turnbull, Martin and Company was a small player in the Federal-Houlder-Shire combination which was dominated by Hughes. Once inside the New Zealand conference

Ayrshire (2) photographed in Wellington harbour by J. Dickie. *[Ian J. Farquhar collection]*

he continually planned to expand his business. It was probably Hughes' influence that led Turnbull, Martin to build the much larger steamer *Ayrshire* in 1903. Federal had built a series of larger refrigerated ships from 1899 and the *Ayrshire* had the same dimensions as the Federal *Suffolk, Essex, Dorset* and *Somerset.* The Shire steamers shared in a pooling agreement for the cargo as well as rationalized sailings and, with uniform freight rates between all lines, Turnbull, Martin and Company was in a much better financial position than at any stage in its history. However, the fortunes of the company were to change forever from 1910 as in that year Cayzer, Irvine and Co. Ltd. of Glasgow, trading as The Clan Line of Steamers, purchased a controlling interest in the company. The Elderslie Steamship Co. Ltd. was wound up and the ownership of the Shire steamers was transferred to a new company – The Scottish Shire Line Ltd. The Sydney brokerage firm of A. Macarthur and Company had been offering a regular monthly service from Sydney and other Australian ports to London, Manchester and Glasgow. For many years the company had used the ships of the Gulf Line Ltd. of Greenock but, when this company fell by the wayside, Macarthur and Company, then trading as Macarthur Shipping and Agency Co. Ltd., invited the Clan Line to fill the gap and the company entered the Australian trade in 1908. It obviously saw the potential of increased pooling rights by the purchase of Turnbull, Martin and from 1911 six Clan Line vessels were built with refrigerated space.

Hughes attempted to purchase Houlder Brothers in 1910 but his approaches were rebuffed by the Houlder family. A year later Houlders were keen to dispose of their interest in the Australian trade to concentrate on the South American service and initially offered the business to the Cayzers. The Glasgow firm declined the offer and in 1912 Houlders found a buyer in the New Zealand Shipping Company. When Sir John Ellerman began picking parcels of shares in the New Zealand company, Hughes decided to make an offer for the company through a share exchange of un-issued stock between Federal and New Zealand Shipping Company, and this was successfully completed in 1912. The resultant aggregation created a company of significant size and Hughes decided to take out the four Houlder steamers and sell them to the Union Steam Ship

Company of New Zealand Ltd. to operate separately. With the Houlder withdrawal, the Federal and Shire Lines continued with six-weekly sailings from Manchester and Liverpool, but with Federal having merged with New Zealand Shipping Company in 1912 the Scottish Shire Line was somewhat out on a limb, and reliant on the strength of its association with Clan Line to protect its share of trade. When Federal ordered two new 12,000 ton vessels, both having a large refrigerated capacity, and also more space for migrants, in 1911 (*Shropshire* and *Wiltshire*) a third identical vessel (*Argyllshire*) was built to the ownership of the Scottish Shire Line Ltd.

The *Fifeshire* was lost in 1911. She was on passage from Adelaide to London via Albany, Western Australia when she ran ashore in thick fog 20 miles south of Cape Guardafui at the mouth of the Gulf of Aden on 9th August and was abandoned as a total loss. No lives were lost in the stranding but gale force winds played havoc with the lifeboats and one went missing with the loss of 24 lives, including ten passengers.

During the First World War *Argyllshire* and *Ayrshire* were requisitioned by the Australian Government as troop transports. *Argyllshire* was fitted out to carry 100 officers, 1,000 other ranks and 397 horses, while the smaller *Ayrshire* could carry 20 officers, 330 other ranks and 297 horses. They were not released from war service until June 1918. The elderly *Ayrshire* had difficulty maintaining speed in convoys while the *Argyllshire* had two lucky escapes from enemy attacks. Two torpedoes missed their mark in an attack off Le Havre on 27th May 1915. She was not so lucky on 5th February 1917 when just off Plymouth she was hit by a torpedo but managed to reach port using the screw shaft which had not been damaged in the explosion.

After *Argyllshire* in 1911 no further ships were built for the company. All the surviving Shire steamers built in the 1890s were sold between 1913 and 1915, leaving only *Argyllshire* and *Ayrshire,* which were insufficient to provide a separate service without the support of the other lines in a pooling arrangement. After Clan Line assumed full ownership from 25th March 1918, Scottish Shire Line names were given to Clan Line 'hand-me-downs', but many years later Shire

Argyllshire at Sydney. *[Ian J. Farquhar collection]*

names were given to the *Perthshire* (1936), *Lanarkshire* (1940), *Stirlingshire* (1946), *Argyllshire* (1956) and *Ayrshire* (1957). When the fleet was set adrift from the Federal-Houlder-Shire restructuring from 1911, the Shire vessels were more often employed on the Australian berth, and between 1913-1928 they only made a total of 17 voyages to New Zealand. Invariably the vessels continued to operate on the original west coast service with Liverpool and Manchester the principal United Kingdom ports of call.

The remaining Shire vessel which had been built for the original company in 1903 was the *Ayrshire.* She survived a further serious fire between Cape Town and Adelaide in August 1925 but in 1926 she was not so fortunate. She was in the Indian Ocean on passage from Brisbane to London on 26th November 1926 when a fire broke out in her coal bunkers while she was in position 8.36 north by 73.29 east. The ship made best speed towards Colombo but the fire intensified, the hold became red hot and the flames rose to 150 feet. The sloop, HMS *Lupin*, which was close by, attempted to tow *Ayrshire* but the rudder was jammed hard-a-port. Within two days the ship was ablaze fore and aft and the masts had collapsed. At this stage there was no prospect of obtaining tugs and HMS *Lupin* was instructed to sink her if necessary. The crew was rescued by the *City of Nagpur* (10,138/1922), and the *Aeneas* (10,058/1910) was also in the area. HMS *Lupin* was finally able to scuttle *Ayrshire*, without the use of gunfire, on 2nd December.

After many years of frustration in dealing with his one-time friend Allan Hughes, James Caird initiated further court action in March 1927 against Hughes, the New Zealand Shipping Company and the Union Steam Ship Company of New Zealand, claiming his company was entitled to a one third pool share from a pooling agreement signed between the parties on 15th April 1912. The case was so complex that even the judge came to remark 'I can hardly understand this'. In the end, after five days of evidence, Caird had to concede that he could not prove he had a binding contract with Hughes and the action was dismissed. The following day, James Caird commenced another legal action seeking a declaration on when a pooling agreement from 30th July 1912 terminated. An earlier action had been started in July 1921 but without resolution. Ships in the original agreement had been requisitioned or lost in the First World War and were replaced by others. Hughes contended the agreement had been frustrated by the war and would have ceased on the sale of *Buteshire* in 1915 - the only Scottish Shire vessel remaining in the pool which was not under requisition. If it was not that time, then it must have been on 25th March 1918 when James Caird went into full partnership with the Cazyers. However, there were so many imponderables that the parties agreed with the judge that the issues would be better decided outside the courtroom. Hughes' subsequent influence as chairman of the New Zealand Shipping Company, and the holder of the largest pool share in the New Zealand/United Kingdom conference, saw him convince all three lines – Shaw, Savill and Albion, New Zealand Shipping and the Commonwealth and Dominion Line – to buy the *Argyllshire* as part settlement of the dispute, with each party paying for the ship in proportion to their respective pool shares. Prior to being taken over by the conference in December 1929, under the management of the Federal Steam Navigation Company, the *Argyllshire* had been laid up from 1926 and after just a few voyages for the new owners again returned to lay up before being purchased by Clan Line in December 1932. The conference lines paid an inflated price of £145,000 in 1929, and she only realised £12,000 when she was sold to Clan Line in 1932.

Whilst he may have lost the Scottish Shire Line to the Clan Line, James Caird used his large fortune to preserve Britain's maritime history. He was the largest contributor to the restoration of HMS *Victory*. But this was minor compared with his involvement with a small group of like-minded people in the development of a national museum for Britain. In 1933 and 1934 Caird funded the cost of refurbishing the former Royal Hospital at Greenwich to create a maritime museum. The National Maritime Museum was opened in 1937 and Caird was one of its greatest benefactors. The museum even holds the builder's model of the pioneering refrigerated steamer *Elderslie,* the first steamer specially built for the New Zealand trade in 1884. James Caird was made a Baronet in 1928 – Sir James Caird of Glenfarquhar. He died in 1954 in his 91st year.

Clan Urquhart, the former *Argyllshire* (2). *[B. and A. Feilden/J. and M. Clarkson collection]*

Perthshire at anchor in Sydney Harbour, still with yards on her foremast (above). The yards had been removed by the time the second photograph was taken, which shows her off Greenwich on charter to British India Steam Navigation Co. Ltd. (middle). The steam pipe attached to the funnel is more obvious in this view. As the third photograph, taken at Malta, shows she was further modified during her 20-year naval career, during which she served as a dummy battleship, oiler and stores' ship (bottom). Further illustrations of *Perthshire* appeared in 'Record' 9, page 42. *[Ian J. Farquhar collection (2); J. and M. Clarkson collection]*

Fleet list, part 2

14. PERTHSHIRE 1893-1914
O.N. 102638 5,550g 3,623n
420.0 x 54.0 x 28.8 feet
T.3-cyl. by R. and W. Hawthorn,
Leslie and Co. Ltd., Hebburn-on-
Tyne; 493 NHP.
12.8.1893: Launched by R. and
W. Hawthorn, Leslie and Co. Ltd.,
Hebburn-on-Tyne (Yard No. 315).
3.11.1893: Registered in the owner-
ship of the Elderslie Steamship Co.
Ltd. (Turnbull, Martin and Co., managers), Glasgow as PERTHSHIRE.
10.8.1910: Transferred to the
Scottish Shire Line Ltd. (Turnbull,
Martin and Co. Ltd., managers),
Glasgow.
28.10.1914: Sold to the Admiralty for
conversion into the dummy battleship
VANGUARD.
1915: Converted to become the
Coaling Officer's ship at Scapa
Flow, carrying canteen stores, fresh
water and fuel and reverted to
PERTHSHIRE.
3.1920: Converted into an oiler.
1922: Converted into a stores carrier.
26.2.1934: Sold to Italy and broken
up by S.A. Cantiere di Portovenere at
La Spezia.
22.3.1934: Register closed.

15. BUTESHIRE (2) 1893-1915

O.N. 102653 5,574g 3,636n
420.0 x 54.0 x 28.7 feet
T.3-cyl. by R. and W. Hawthorn, Leslie and Co. Ltd., Hebburn-on-Tyne; 600 NHP, 3,000 IHP, 11.5 knots.
10.10.1893: Launched by R. and W. Hawthorn, Leslie and Co. Ltd., Hebburn-on-Tyne (Yard No. 316).
22.12.1893: Registered in the ownership of the Elderslie Steamship Co. Ltd. (Turnbull, Martin and Co., managers), Glasgow as BUTESHIRE.
10.8.1910: Transferred to the Scottish Shire Line Ltd. (Turnbull, Martin and Co. Ltd., managers), Glasgow.
19.4.1915: Sold to the Bollington Grange Steamship Co. Ltd. (Houlder Brothers and Co. Ltd., managers), London.
21.4.1915: Renamed BOLLINGTON GRANGE.
29.9.1915: Transferred to Furness-Houlder Argentine Lines Ltd., London.
26.1.1916: Renamed CANONESA.
1.5.1918: Torpedoed and damaged by the German submarine UB 57 off Worthing with the loss of eight lives. Brought into Southampton Water and abandoned to the British Government as war loss insurers.
22.10.1918: Owners became the Shipping Controller, London.
1.11.1918: Register closed.
17.12.1919: Registered in the ownership of the Brodway Steamship Co. Ltd. (Blue Star Line Ltd., managers), London as MAGICSTAR.
14.4.1920: Transferred to the Union Cold Storage Co. Ltd. (Blue Star Line (1920) Ltd., managers), London.
20.5.1930: Managers became Blue Star Line Ltd.
1930: Sold to T.W. Ward Ltd., Sheffield and broken up at Inverkeithing.
13.6.1930: Register closed.

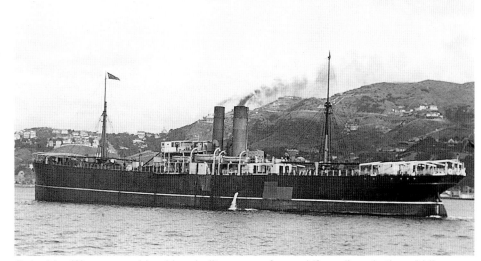

Buteshire (2) was considerably rebuilt during her career. As seen in the top photograph, taken at Sydney, her hull has wells fore and aft similar to her near-sister *Perthshire*, and she has an uptake for her donkey boiler immediately in front of the funnel. It is said that the owners regarded this pipe as ugly, and at some point it was replaced with a more substantial forward 'funnel', as in the middle photograph also at Sydney and the bottom one, at Wellington. However, these photographs also show other changes, as her wells have been filled in and the bridge structure rebuilt. Did this rebuilding occur after one of the fires she suffered? *[Ian J. Farquhar collection (all three)]*

The top right photograph shows *Buteshire* (2) after her sale to Houlder Brothers as *Bollington Grange*. Further renamed *Canonesa* she was torpedoed by a German submarine in the English Channel in May 1918 causing the loss of eight lives and extensive damage to the ship. When rebuilt by Blue Star as *Magicstar* she lost the forward funnel (middle right photograph). *[Ian J. Farquhar collection (both)]*

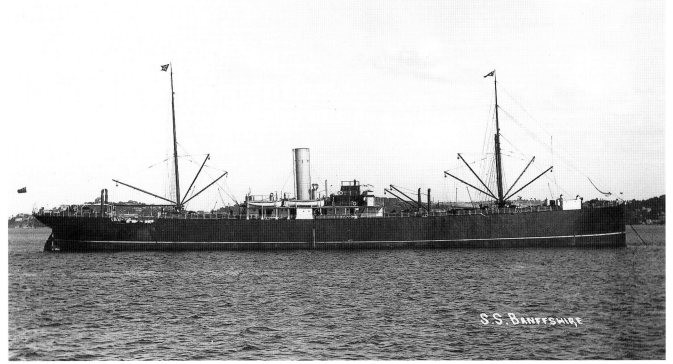

Banffshire at Sydney. *[J. Dickie/Roy Fenton collection]*

16. BANFFSHIRE 1894-1915
O.N. 104587 5,526g 3,603n
420.0 x 54.0 x 28.7 feet
T.3-cyl. by R. and W. Hawthorn, Leslie and Co. Ltd., Hebburn-on-Tyne; 380 NHP, 3,000 IHP, 11.75 knots.
1.9.1894: Launched by R. and W. Hawthorn, Leslie and Co. Ltd., Hebburn-on-Tyne (Yard No. 324).

10.11.1894: Registered in the ownership of the Elderslie Steamship Co. Ltd. (Turnbull, Martin and Co., managers), Glasgow as BANFFSHIRE.
26.4.1910: Transferred to the Scottish Shire Line Ltd. (Turnbull, Martin and Co. Ltd., managers), Glasgow.
7.6.1915: Sold to Brodness Steamship

Co. Ltd. (Blue Star Line Ltd., managers), London.
9.6.1915: Renamed BRODNESS.
31.3.1917: Torpedoed and sunk by the German submarine UC 38 five miles west north west of Port Anzio whilst on a voyage from Genoa to Port Said.
11.5.1917: Register closed.

Banffshire at Wellington. *[J. Dickie/Ian J. Farquhar collection]*

17. MORAYSHIRE (2) 1898-1915
O.N. 108778 5,576g 3,597n
420.0 x 54.0 x 28.6 feet
T.3-cyl. by R. and W. Hawthorn, Leslie and Co. Ltd., Hebburn-on-Tyne; 430 NHP.
1.9.1898: Launched by R. and W. Hawthorn, Leslie and Co. Ltd., Hebburn-on-Tyne (Yard No. 359).
10.12.1898: Registered in the ownership of the Elderslie Steamship Co. Ltd. (Turnbull, Martin and Company, managers), Glasgow as MORAYSHIRE.
10.8.1910: Transferred to the Scottish Shire Line Ltd. (Turnbull, Martin and Co. Ltd., managers), Glasgow.
30.3.1915: Sold to the Brodliffe Steamship Co. Ltd. (Blue Star Line Ltd., managers), London.
31.3.1915: Renamed BRODLIFFE.
14.4.1920: Transferred to the Union Cold Storage Co. Ltd. (Blue Star Line (1920) Ltd., managers), London.
24.6.1920: Renamed TUSCANSTAR.
13.3.1929: Register closed on sale to Fratelli Rizzuto, Italy, and renamed FORTUNSTAR.
1936: Sold to Ignazio Messina and C., Genoa, Italy and renamed SEMIEN.
10.6.1940: Seized at Dakar when Italy invaded France, but handed back to owners after the Franco-German Armistice.
1942: Sold to Nautilus S.A. (Swiss Shipping Co. Ltd., managers), Basle, Switzerland and renamed LUGANO.
1948: Resold to Ignazio Messina and C., Genoa, Italy.
30.7.1952: Delivered at Savona for demolition by ARDEM S.p.A.

Seen at Port Chalmers, *Morayshire* (2) narrowly missed being the first vessel to have its refrigerating machinery classed by Lloyd's Register. Given the dire consequences to a cargo of frozen meat from break down of a refrigeration system, such surveying and classification had been called for by meat shippers, insurers and ship owners. In the event, Lund's *Wakool* (5,004/1898) was the first ship to receive the notation '*RMC' in the register book in December 1898, *Morayshire* being the second a few days later. *[De Maus/K. O'Donoghue collection]*

Fifeshire (3). Two out of the three ships carrying this name were wrecked, the third coming to grief on Cape Guardafui near where, 54 years later, the *Ayrshire* (9,360/1957) was to become Clan Line's final casualty. *[Ian J. Farquhar collection]*

18. FIFESHIRE (3) 1898-1911
O.N. 108775 5,672g 3,628n
420.5 x 54.7 x 28.8 feet
T.3-cyl. by the Clydebank Engineering and Shipbuilding Co. Ltd., Clydebank; 309 NHP, 3,000 IHP, 11 knots.
15.10.1898: Launched by Clydebank Engineering and Shipbuilding Co. Ltd., Clydebank (Yard No. 332).

5.12.1898: Registered in the ownership of the Elderslie Steamship Co. Ltd. (Turnbull, Martin and Co. Ltd., managers), Glasgow as FIFESHIRE.
10.8.1910: Transferred to the Scottish Shire Line Ltd. (Turnbull, Martin and Co. Ltd., managers), Glasgow.
9.8.1911: Stranded in fog 20 miles south of Cape Guardafui, Gulf of Aden whilst on a

voyage from Sydney, New South Wales to the United Kingdom with general cargo.
11.8.1911: Abandoned in deteriorating weather. 24 lives were lost.
14.8.1911: Declared a constructive total loss.
28.10.1911: Register closed.

Nairnshire (2) at Sydney (above) and also photographed on the Mersey as *Gothicstar* (opposite page top) in Blue Star ownership during the 1920s, and with the name spelt *Gothic Star* in the 1930s (opposite page middle). Note the subtle changes in hull and funnel colours which have taken place between the two photographs opposite. *[William Livermore/Ian J. Farquhar collection; B. and A. Feilden/J. and M. Clarkson; John McRoberts/J. and M. Clarkson]*

19. NAIRNSHIRE (2) 1899-1915

O.N. 108793 5,673g 3,628n
420.5 x 54.7 x 28.8 feet
T.3-cyl. by the Clydebank Engineering and Shipbuilding Co. Ltd., Clydebank; 309 NHP, 3,000 IHP, 11 knots.
16.12.1898: Launched by Clydebank Engineering and Shipbuilding Co. Ltd., Clydebank (Yard No. 333).
15.2.1899: Registered in the ownership of the Elderslie Steamship Co. Ltd. (Turnbull, Martin and Co. Ltd., managers), Glasgow as NAIRNSHIRE.
2.1899: Completed.
10.8.1910: Transferred to the Scottish Shire Line Ltd. (Turnbull, Martin and Co. Ltd., managers), Glasgow.
2.6.1915: Sold to the Brodholme Steamship Co. Ltd. (Blue Star Line Ltd., managers), London
4.6.1915: Renamed BRODHOLME.
24.11.1920: Transferred to the Union Cold Storage Co. Ltd. (Blue Star Line (1920) Ltd., managers), London.
5.5.1921: Renamed GOTHICSTAR.
2.9.1929: Transferred to Blue Star Line (1920) Ltd., London.
20.5.1930: Transferred to Blue Star Line Ltd., London.
4.10.1929: Renamed GOTHIC STAR.
4.6.1938: Register closed on sale to Italian breakers.
4.7.1938: Arrived at Savona to be broken up.

20. AYRSHIRE (2) 1903-1926

O.N. 119066 9,188g 5,931n
460.0 x 58.8 x 31.8 feet
Two x T.3-cyl. by the North Eastern Marine Engineering Co. Ltd., Newcastle-upon-Tyne driving twin screws; 893 NHP total, 13 knots.
28.8.1903: Launched by R. and W. Hawthorn, Leslie and Co. Ltd., Newcastle-upon-Tyne (Yard No. 389).
10.11.1903: Registered in the ownership of the D'Arcy M. Dawes and David C. Leck, London (Turnbull, Martin and Co. Ltd., Glasgow, managers) as AYRSHIRE.
23.6.1908: Transferred to the Elderslie Steamship Co. Ltd. (Turnbull, Martin and Co., managers), Glasgow.
10.8.1910: Transferred to the Scottish Shire Line Ltd. (Turnbull, Martin and Co. Ltd., managers), Glasgow.
28.11.1926: Abandoned on fire in the Indian Ocean in position 07.50 north by 73.50 east whilst on a voyage from Brisbane to U.K. and the Continent with general cargo including tallow and frozen

Ayrshire (2) at Adelaide. *[Ian J. Farquhar collection]*

general cargo including tallow and frozen meat. The crew was rescued by the *City of Nagpur* (10,138/1922) and the *Aeneas* (10,058/1910).

2.12.1926: Scuttled in position 09.12 north by 73.28 east by HMS *Lupin*.
17.12.1926: Register closed.

21. ARGYLLSHIRE (2) 1911-1929

O.N. 129581 10,236g 6,054n
526.2 x 61.4 x 33.3 feet
Two Q.4-cyl. by John Brown and Co. Ltd., Clydebank driving twin screws; 644 NHP, 5,500 IHP, 14 knots.

27.2.1911: Launched by John Brown and Co. Ltd., Clydebank (Yard No. 399).
6.1911: Completed.
1.7.1911: Registered in the ownership of the Scottish Shire Line (Turnbull, Martin and Co. Ltd., managers), Glasgow as ARGYLLSHIRE.
2.2.1917: Torpedoed about three miles off Start Point, but succeeded in reaching Falmouth. Later repaired.

7.10.1929: Sold to the Federal Steam Navigation Co. Ltd., London.
15.11.1932: Sold to The Clan Line Steamers Ltd. (Cayzer, Irvine and Co. Ltd., managers), Glasgow for £12,000.
21.12.1932: Renamed CLAN URQUHART.
1936: Sold to T.W. Ward Ltd., Sheffield for breaking up
30.10.1936: Arrived at Briton Ferry.
14.3.1937: During demolition damaged by fire and scuttled in shallow water.
12.10.1937: Register closed.

Argyllshire at Adelaide. *[Ian J. Farquhar collection]*

SOURCES AND ACKNOWLEDGEMENTS

We thank all who gave permission for their photographs to be used, and for help in finding photographs we are particularly grateful to Tony Smith, Jim McFaul and David Whiteside of the World Ship Photo Library; to Ian Farquhar, F.W. Hawks, Peter Newall, William Schell, George Scott; and to David Hodge and Bob Todd of the National Maritime Museum, and other museums and institutions listed.

Research sources have included the *Registers* of William Schell and Tony Starke, *Lloyd's Register, Lloyd's Confidential Index, Lloyd's War Losses, Mercantile Navy Lists, Marine News* and *Shipbuilding and Shipping Record*. Use of the facilities of the World Ship Society, the Guildhall Library, the National Archives and Lloyd's Register of Shipping and the help of Dr Malcolm Cooper are gratefully acknowledged. Particular thanks also to Heather Fenton for editorial and indexing work, and to Marion Clarkson for accountancy services.

Photographer in Focus: Robert Moffat Scott
Many thanks to Peter Mellier for his detailed description of the time he knew Moffat Scott and to Robert Pabst and Brian Ingpen for their help in preparing this article. Moffat Scott's photo is by courtesy of the Ship Society of South Africa, and the samples of his flag and funnel drawings by courtesy of the World Ship Society Ltd. and its ships' liveries custodian, J.L.Loughran.

Veteran British-built Tugs
Cory Towage Ltd. A Group History by W.J. Harvey (World Ship Society, 2000), *Blow Five, A History of Alexandra Towing Co. Ltd.*, by W.B. Hallam (The Journal of Commerce and Shipping Telegraph Ltd., 1976). Particular thanks to David Hazell, Felixstowe, and to Andrew Wiltshire and Kevin Blair.

OVERSEAS FRUIT SHIPS IN HOBART 1960-1976: Part 2

Rex Cox

NESTOR

Caledon Shipbuilding and Engineering Co. Ltd., Dundee, 1952; 7,802gt, 490 feet.
Three steam turbines double-reduction geared to a single screw by Metropolitan Vickers Electrical Co. Ltd., Manchester.
Blue Funnel liners loaded fruit for both European and South East Asian destinations during the 1960s. Registered in the ownership of the Ocean Steam Ship Co. Ltd., *Nestor* was on the latter berth between 1963 and 1968, and would also take any other cargoes offering. She is shown here returning to the Hobart wharves from Risdon, having lifted a consignment of zinc.

Transferred to Glen Line in 1968 as *Glenaffric,* she returned to Blue Funnel as *Orestes* two years later. Sold foreign as *Aegis Dignity* in 1971, she was delivered to breakers at Whampoa towards the end of 1973.

The previous *Nestor,* completed in 1913, was famous for her huge funnel, which towered some 75 feet above the superstructure.

COOLAROO

Eriksbergs M/V A/B, Gothenburg, 1956; 5,775gt, 433 feet.
6-cyl. 2SCSA Burmeister & Wain-type oil engine by Eriksbergs M/V A/B, Gothenburg.
Coolaroo was the first of several

specialized fruit carriers which came to Hobart from 1956 onwards under the auspices of Rederi A/B Transatlantic, Gothenburg; others were *Cooranga* (3,711/55) and *Coolgardie* (3,334/56). They stood out from the crowd amongst the traditional cargo liners then dominating the trade.

Registered in the name of Rederi A/B Transmark (G. Carlsson, manager), Gothenburg, *Coolaroo* ran aground off Helsinki on 27th October 1961, while outward bound in ballast for Rostock, East Germany. She later broke in two, with the forepart sinking.

She is shown here arriving in Hobart the previous year, on 10th April 1960.

CAYMAN
Eriksbergs M/V A/B, Gothenburg, 1956;
6,192gt, 444 feet.
7-cyl. 2SCSA Burmeister & Wain-type
oil engine by Eriksbergs M/V A/B,
Gothenburg.
Owned by Rederi A/B Salenia (Sven
Salén A/B), Stockholm, *Cayman*
presented a similar appearance to
Coolaroo, though her dimensions were
slightly larger.
　　　Pictured in afternoon sunlight
on 2nd April 1967, she was renamed

Cabo Bolinao in 1971 and broken up at
Hong Kong in 1984.

ANTIGUA
Öresundsvarvet A/B, Landskrona, 1960;
8,288gt, 493 feet.
Two steam turbines double-reduction
geared to a single screw by Turbin A/B
De Laval, Ljungström.
Antigua was an early morning arrival
on 20th April 1965, one of five Salén
reefers to load in Hobart that season.
She took fruit for Gothenburg, Malmö,

Stockholm and Helsinki. Also visible
is the stern of the American research
vessel *Robert D. Conrad* (1,300/1962).
　　　Salén sold *Antigua* in 1972 to
Transoceanic Reefers Line Inc., Liberia,
as *Antilla*. She became *Antartide* in
1977 and *Rio* in 1978 under Liberian
registry. A brief spell under the Italian
flag as *Rosy* followed in 1979 and
1980, then she was renamed *Safina*
Reefer for Saudi Arabian interests
before arriving at Gadani Beach on 28th
February 1983 for demolition.

HERBORG

Oresundsvarvet A/B, Landskrona, 1950;
3,312gt, 341 feet.
10-cyl. 2SCSA oil engine by A/B
Götaverken, Gothenburg.
Arriving on 31st May 1966 to take fruit
for Hull only, *Herborg* had been owned
since 1958 by Vaboens Rederi A/S
(Olaf Vaboen), Kristiansand. She was
built for another Norwegian owner, C.H.
Sorensen and Sons, as *Viator.*
Herborg was sold to Uruguay in 1970
as *Zorzal*, being renamed *Estemar II*
three years later. Her owners dropped
the numerals and hoisted the flag of
Panama in 1980, presumably as a
prelude to disposal because *Estemar*
anchored off Karachi on 7th December
that year following sale to Pakistani
breakers.

STELLA MARINA

Kockums M/V A/B, Malmö, 1950;
3,850gt, 398 feet.
8-cyl. 2SCDA oil engine by Kockums
M/V A/B, Malmö.
Owned by Stockholms Rederi A/B
Svea (Curt Högberg), Stockholm, and
photographed berthing in Hobart on a
very wet 14th May 1964, *Stella Marina*
was the first of many reefers to visit the
port under Salén charter over the next
decade.

    Stella Marina became
Somalia when sold to the Italian flag
later in 1964, then *Crown Fruit* in 1973
for Universal Seaways Private Ltd.,
Singapore. A fire broke out on 3rd
March 1976 while she was in dry dock
at the Hiroshima yard of Kanawa Dock
Co. Ltd.; it caused serious damage to
the after section of the ship and she
was considered beyond repair. Sold to
Taiwan breakers, she left Hiroshima on
22nd May 1976 in tow for Kaohsiung.

CHUNG THAI

Burmeister & Wain, Copenhagen, 1939;
3,352gt, 337 feet.
10-cyl. 2SCSA oil engine by Burmeister
& Wain, Copenhagen.

Arriving on 6th May 1968 to load 67,000 cases of apples for Manila, *Chung Thai* was a ship of many previous names, but was then nearing the end of a career spent under five national flags; in fact, her sale for breaking up in Taiwan was reported the following November. During her stay in Hobart all cargo gear had to be inspected and certified before loading could commence.

Like *Stella Marina* she carried the name *Somalia* for part of her career; in fact, both vessels are listed in 1965 'Lloyd's Register' under this name and the ownership of Societa Siciliana Servizi Marittimi S.p.A., Palermo.

Launched as *Prinsdal*, she had been completed as *Ahrensburg* for Harald Schuldt & Co. K.G., Hamburg. 1946 saw her taken over by the Norwegian Government and placed under Thor Dahl management, first as *Asnes* but then with the more appropriate name of *Thornes*. Acquired during the following year by Alf Torgersen, Oslo, she operated as *Mona Lisa* until 1956. Then came nine years under the Italian flag as *Somalia* before a brief stint as *Chenchang* for a company domiciled in Taiwan. 1966 saw her changing hands for the last time, and it was Chung Lien Navigation Co. S.A., Panama, which disposed of her to the breakers not long after this Hobart visit.

POLAR PARAGUAY

Blohm and Voss A.G., Hamburg, 1968;
5,637gt, 485 feet.
Two 16-cyl. 4SCSA Pielstick-type oil
engines geared to a single screw by
Ottensener Eisenwerke, Hamburg.
Owned by Hamburg-Südamerikanische D.G., West Germany, but shown here on a Salén charter in March 1971. Four of her five sisters also loaded fruit in Hobart at various times.

Polar Paraguay towed her owner's container ship *Columbus New Zealand* (19,146/1971) to Balboa after the latter suffered an engine room fire on 20th December 1974 when near the Galapagos Islands.

She was sold to the Uiterwyk Corporation in 1977, placed under the Liberian flag and chartered back to Hamburg-Süd for five years. Similar arrangements applied to all the sister ships, though their later careers diverged in some cases.

Sold in 1982 to Greek owners without change of name, she was then purchased at auction by Panamanian interests in 1986 and renamed *Frio Mexico*. She arrived at Alang for breaking up on 11th February 1993.

TOLOA
Gulf Ship Building Corporation,
Chickasaw, 1945; 6,732gt, 455 feet.
Four steam turbines double-reduction
geared to two screw shafts by De Laval
Steam Turbine Co., Trenton.
Loaded down to her marks, *Toloa* is
leaving Hobart on 27th April 1970.
She had only just been renamed for
Caraibische Scheepvaart Maatschappij
N.V., Netherlands, prior to this visit,
having operated formerly as United
Fruit's *Esparta* under the US flag.
Sister ship *Talamanca* (6,729/1945) ex
Limon arrived two weeks later, while five
more reefers associated with the Fyffes

Group also loaded at Hobart during that
particular fruit export season.
    Toloa had a good career
of some 32 years until her arrival at
Kaohsiung on 18th June 1977 for
demolition.

REEFER CITY
Krögerwerft G.m.b.H., Rendsburg,
1962; 3,505gt, 390 feet.
Two 10-cyl. 4SCSA oil engines
with flexible coupling and single-
reduction gearing to the screw shaft
by Maschinenbau Augsburg-Nürnberg,
Hamburg.
Reefer Lines of Singapore built up a

fleet of small but interesting second
hand vessels in the early 1970s,
acquiring them from Danish, West
German and British owners. *Reefer*
City was the former *Baltic Sun* of United
Baltic Corporation Ltd., and was still
wearing their grey hull when she first
arrived in Hobart on 21st May 1973.
    Registered in the name of
Reefer City (Private) Ltd., Singapore, she
is seen here almost two years later (13th
April 1975) preparing to take another
cargo for the East. In the background,
Port St. Lawrence (9,040/1961) was
also loading fruit. *Reefer City* arrived at
Kaohsiung on 21st January 1983.

The above photo was bought from an American source who described it as being of an unidentified British steamer. Imagine my delight when the picture arrived, not only was the quality of the photo excellent but the ship was in camouflage and her name was clearly displayed on the bridge front - *Lycaon*. Despite her war-worn appearance *Lycaon* was still almost new having been completed in 1913 by R. and W. Hawthorn, Leslie and Co. Ltd. at Hebburn. She survived both world wars and finally went to the breakers in 1952 as the *Gleniffer*. Looking at the other craft in the picture the photo was most likely taken in the United States.

Old pictures of shipping on the Thames always intrigue me. Not so much the individual craft but the variety and quantity of traffic on the river. In this view, taken in the 1880s perhaps, there are many barges in the foreground and more further back, also some sailing barges near to the Tower of London. Look at the old steam paddle tug belching smoke in mid-river and note the shape of her bow. If only we knew her name. There are various coasters and short sea traders both alongside and in the stream. Just one vessel is identifiable - the one on the right could be *Fyenoord*. Is the nearest coaster on the left one of Langlands?

FROM THE BOSUN'S LOCKER
John Clarkson

From time to time we come across odd photographs which are outstanding in some way, perhaps the quality of the picture or the content. If we have articles in preparation where they can be used we put them to one side but often there is no prospect of using them. Two such pictures are reproduced opposite. The first for its content and quality and the second for the sheer amount of shipping portrayed.

Due to a lack of space in 'Record 39' replies relating to photos earlier issues of 'Record' had to be held over. Not a totally bad thing as more comments on some pictures were received after publication.

2/38. There have been three suggestions as to the identity of this ship, all correspondents agreeing that it is a former Norddeutscher Lloyd vessel used as a transport or hospital ship in the Dardanelles. Robert H. Langlois has painstakingly compared this photograph with those of the NDL ships of this class. After carefully looking at the dates each was involved in the Gallipoli campaign and detailed differences especially around the stern, he concludes that it was taken between the end of April and early July 1915 and depicts the British Expeditionary Force Transport *Lützow* (8,818/1908), which was renamed *Huntsend* in mid 1915. Captain Peter H. King concurs in so far that it is either *Huntsend* or her sister *Derfflinger* which became *Huntsgreen* (9,060/1908). Both *Lutzow* and *Derfflinger* were seized by Britain near Port Said in August 1914. However, Ian Farquhar begs to differ. He suggests the ship is the *Tras Os Montes* which was built in 1906 as the NDL's *Bülow*. She was seized by Portugal on 24th February 1916 having been in Lisbon since August 1914. She was renamed *Tras Os Montes* under the management of Transportes Maritimos do Estado, Lisbon and placed under the British Shipping Controller. *Tras Os Montes* carried invalided troops back to Australia in 1919 and was returned to Portugal following the war, remaining under Portuguese ownership and being renamed *Nyassa* in 1924 after a major refit. She was broken up by Hughes Bolckow at Blyth from the end of 1951.

The pennant number A 25 proved something of a red herring. For the first Imperial Convoy from Australia this number was allocated to the *Anglo Egyptian* (7,379/1912), a freighter belonging to the Nitrate Producers' Steamship Co. Ltd., which still had this pennant number in the 20th Imperial Convoy from Australia. The ship in the photograph is clearly not *Anglo Egyptian*, so the pennant numbers must have been re-activated, and this lends support to Ian's suggestion that it is a post-war view. However, the ship in photograph 2/38 definitely flies the Red Ensign, whilst 'Lloyd's Register' for both 1919 and 1920 shows *Tras Os Montes* as being under the Portugese flag. Whilst the case is not yet closed, the balance of probability is that the ship depicted is *Lutzow*.

4/38. Bill Schell is adamant that this ship is certainly not, as suggested, *Marco* ex *Capac* – that vessel had deck erections which make her a three islander. He suggests the photo shows the Italian *Norge* (6,534/1907), originally Tyser's *Whakarua*, then *Port Hacking*. Another possibility is *Capo Nord* (also ex-Tyser, in this case the former *Mimiro*, 6,225/1900), but the name *Norge* fits better– five letters and more or less the same shape as the name *Marco*. The only noticeable difference Bill can see between this photo and Raul Maya's negatives of *Norge* taken in 1938 is that the crow's nest looks bigger in the latter. Both *Norge* and *Capo Norte* were owned by Andrea Zanchi of

Genoa and his funnel – blue base with white band below black top – certainly fits with that in the photograph.

7/38. J.W. Grainger believes the vessel nearest the camera is Shaw, Savill's *Tokomaru* (6,238/1893, ex *Westmeath*), owned from 1893 to 1915, or the same company's *Aotea* (6,363/1894). Duncan Haws drawings in 'Merchant Fleets 10' suggest that *Tokomaru* is the more likely. He goes on to speculate that the vessel alongside is the same company's *Kumara* (6,034/1899) or her sister *Waiwera* (6,237/1899). He suggests that the location is the Shaw, Savill berth in the Royal Albert Dock, London.

The non-existent *Eston*

Christy MacHale asks for readers' help in solving a problem. He has a photograph showing a ship which has no existence in the Starke/Schell registers. She is described as the 'Furness Liner *Eston*', and Christy supposes she is at Fowey. From the placard under the after boat on her port side proclaiming 'Belgian Relief Rotterdam' he guesses the picture dates from early in the First World War, when the idea was to send supplies to invaded Belgium via the neutral Netherlands. But the *Eston* doesn't feature in the registers (the only vessel of the name is P&O's war-built *Eston*, but she is a very different-looking ship). However, in his book on Furness Withy, David Burrell adds a note to his entry on the *South Point* of 1912 (lost 27th March 1915) implying that she was *laid down* as the *Eston*. Trouble is, what is in Christy's photograph is manifestly a *completed* ship. Has anyone ideas or (even better) explanations?

The non-photographed *Barnby*

Another plea for help comes from Merlin Dexter. He bought at auction a builder's model of Rowland and Marwood's *Barnby* of 1940. She was the last of four steam tramps with Maierform bows built by Short Brothers Ltd. at Sunderland and which were ordered by Chapman and Willan of Newcastle-upon-Tyne, who sold the fourth to the Whitby company before completion. Merlin believes that because she was built during wartime there were no launch or trials photographs taken of *Barnby*, and none of her in service as she was torpedoed in the North Atlantic in May 1941. If so, his builder's model is the only record of the ship, although photographs exist of each of her sisters *Generton*, *Hermiston* and *Scorton* which survived the war. Do any readers know if *Barnby* was, in fact, photographed during her short life?

A plea to British readers

That ramshackle organisation the British Post Office, who call themselves the Royal Mail, have recently changed the way they price letters. An envelope of A4 size or larger now costs slightly more than one smaller than A4. Fair enough, but they impose a fine of £1 on those to whom are sent letters with insufficient postage. It beggars belief that an organisation renowned for its ability to lose, delay, damage and have stolen letters entrusted to its care (and to go to almost any length to deny liability) should start to punish its innocent customers in this way. And to add injury to insult, the unfortunate non-recipient may well have to travel some distance and queue in order to collect the said underpaid item, often at an office where it is impossible to park. So, we would ask British readers who correspond with us to be aware that an A4 letter (that's the size of this journal) up to 100gm will cost 44p first class (which means there's a chance it might be delivered the next day) and 37p second class.

1/40 On the back is written '*Meremba* beached at Dover'. *Meremba* we cannot find and from enlarging the bow section some of the letters could be *-ca-uec*. Has anyone any ideas as to the ship and the occasion?

2/40 Nothing on the back of this card of an attractive smallish passenger/cargo steamer. The name may be written on the front but is almost illegible. If so it is two words, the first being *Teh* and the second may start with an *S*.

3/40 This photograph has even less information: 'English steamer on fire'. Closer examination reveals the bridge is burnt out and the funnel may have been a light colour with a dark top. There is what looks like a tug or salvage ship on her starboard side.

4/40 David Whiteside submitted the above picture of *Mercator* taken at Preston in 1966 whilst discharging a cargo of petrol from the continent. The ship cannot be found in 'Lloyd's Register' and any information on her would be appreciated. It is possible that *Mercator* was listed elsewhere, as an inland waterways craft perhaps and her appearance supports this theory. If this is so, how could such a craft be allowed to make loaded coastwise voyages?

5/40. Regular contributor John B. Hill sent this photograph which he took in La Spezia during August 1978 (left). He asks for identification of the tug, which he thinks is named *Santa Maria*, but which is not in 'Lloyd's Register' under this name.

6/40 In looking through some United States Coast Guard photographs taken in New York harbour during the Second World War, Ian Farquhar came across this image of the *Empire Spray* (below), one of the 35 CAM ships (catapult merchant ship). Abaft the funnel appears a metal latticework structure. Maybe it was an early experiment with radio or radar antennas. Can any reader advise what the structure was for?

7/40 Another tug query comes from Michael Cassar, who enlarged a portion of a photograph of another ship to show this salvage tug visiting Malta some years ago. Can anyone identify it?

EVERY PICTURE...

Ian Wilson supplied this fine photograph, but has no idea where it was taken. Apart from the interest in the ships, the foreground has much to ponder over, including the white-coated and contemplative overseer (is that a solar topi he is wearing?), the seated gentlemen apparently repairing the quay, the stacks of ingots, and the various sturdy and largely horse-drawn vehicles.

The steamer *Beckenham* (4,566/1901) in the foreground provides few indications as to the date or whereabouts of the photograph. She was built by Ropner and Son at Stockton-on-Tees for the British Steamship Co. Ltd. of Watts, Watts and Co., London and served them all her days until broken up at Genoa in 1931.

However, the more distant ship may give a clue if our identification is correct. The second part of the name is 'Fell' and the most likely candidate is the *Myra Fell* (3,024/1907) built by Irvine's Shipbuilding and Dry Dock Co., Ltd., West Hartlepool for Hessler Shipping Co. Ltd. (J. Hessler and Co. Ltd., managers), Sydney, New South Wales. The funnel colours appear correct for Hessler: red base, white band and black top. This ownership strongly

suggests an Australasian port, or one in the far east.

In 1915 *Myra Fell* was sold to Globe Shipping Co. Ltd. (Humphries (Cardiff), Ltd., managers), Cardiff and two years later renamed *Glodale*. She was wrecked on 1st January 1918 at Point Pogan, six miles west of Cape Syet, Murman Coast whilst on a voyage from Archangel to Middlesbrough.

So, the likelihood is a port in or near Australia, between 1907 and 1915. Can any reader suggest which one?

INDEX TO RECORD 37 TO 40
Issue numbers are shown in bold

Index of ships

All ships' names are listed, including proposed or other names not actually used, which are shown in brackets.

Duchess of Bedford 37:61
Duguesclin 39:168
Duke of Fife 39:169
Duke of Norfolk 39:167,169-70
Duke of Portland 39:167,170
Dundee 37:5;38:78-9
Dunedin 39:165
Dunstan 37:61
Durango (1944) 39:177
Durango (1953) 39:177
Durham 39:172
Dymas 38:110
E.S. Styetler (tug) 40:226
Eagle 37:54
Eastern Concord 38:117
Eastham (tug) 37:39
Eccles (tug) 37:38
Ecctonia 37:15,17
Eden 39:168
Edmundson (HMCS) 39:190;40:233
Effigyny 38:80
Efthalia Mari 39:138
Egnatia 37:60
Egret (1903) 37:4,7
Egret (1937) 38:75-6
Egret (1958) 37:5;38:80-1;39:183
Eiko Maru 40:230
Eilean Eisdeal 39:186
Eland 38:96
Elderslie 39:166,168-9;40:239,243
Eldesa 39:186
Elevator No.5 39:159
Elginshire (1882)39:165,168
Elginshire (1891) 39:170-1
Elias 40:199,209
Elisabeth (barge) 39:163
Elizabeth Howard (tug) 37:34;40:218
Ellamy 39:169
Ellet (USS) 39:192
Elli 2 38:121
Empire Buckler 40:235
Empire Captain 39:150
Empire Chief 38:109
Empire Clarion 39:148
Empire Collins 37:58
Empire Damsel 39:156
Empire Dickens 39:149
Empire Factor 39:155
Empire Goodwin 37:59
Empire Governor 37:50;38:106
Empire Halladale 38:110
Empire Ken 38:110
Empire Life 39:150
Empire Macrac 40:230
Empire Mayring 38:82-3;39:184;40:236
Empire Mayrover 40:236
Empire Maysong 38:82;39:184;40:236
Empire Mortimer 40:235
Empire Palm (tug) 39:158
Empire Rennie 38:117-8
Empire Rosa (tug) 39:162
Empire Spaniel 39:158
Empire Spray 40:259
Empire Test 37:52
Empire Trent 40:231
Empire Waveney 37:50;38:107
Empire Wessex 39:176
Empress of Canada 39:181
Empress of China 37:63
Empress of France 37:49;38:102
Empress of India 37:61,63
Empress of Japan 37:63
Emsland 39:162
Enchantress 37:45
Endymion 39:132,135
English Prince 38:84
Englishman (tug) 38:107
Enmore 37:60
Erica 40:229
Ermland 39:139
Erna 39:153

Esneh 40:194
Esparta 40:255
Espiegle (HMS) 39:156
Esquilino 37:50;38:106
Essex (1902) 37:41;38:83;40:242
Esso Appalachee 39:149
Esso Montgomery (barge) 39:153
Esso Stafford (barge) 39:153
Estemar 40:253
Estemar II 40:253
Eston 40:257
Etrib 40:194
Eucadia 37:22,31
Eudocia 40:200,210
Eugene 40:205
Eun Bong 37:10
Ever Access 37:10
Ever Bright 37:10
Express Hercules 38:100
Express Hyphestos 38:100
Fantome (yacht) 38:106
Far East 37:10
Fares Reefer 38:86,88-9
Farid Fares 38:88
Favel 37:25
Fendris 39:135
Ferdinand Melsom 37:42
Fernvalley 39:150
Ferocia 39:186
Fiducia H 39:186
Fiery Cross (tug) 40:220
Fifeshire (1878) 39:166,168
Fifeshire (1887) 39:169
Fifeshire (1898) 40:239,241-2,248
Finax 38:84
Finisterre (HMS) 39:156
Finnieston 38:112
Fiona 38:67
Fisgard IV (HMS) 38:106
Fleetwood (dredger) 38:104
Flintshire 39:165
Floating Crane No.2 39:164
Florida (tug) 37:45;38:84
Fluellen 39:160
Flying Cock (tug) 40:217
Flying Eagle (tug) 39:189
Flying Falcon (tug) 39:189
Flying Mist (tug) 40:219
Folk On 38:70
Foremost 38 (barge) 39:157
Forest Holme 37:39
Fort Camosun 39:190-2
Fort Mumford 39:191
Fortune Sea 37:10
Fortunstar 40:247
Fos 38:115
Foylemore (tug) 40:217
Frankenfels 38:119
Frankenland 37:55;39:162
Frans Hals 38:118
Frederick (USS) 37:59
Frey 40:227
Frio Mexico 40:254
Fude 37:10
Fulmar 37:4;38:66-7
Furious (HMS) 37:49,51;38:107
Fusilier 37:47
Fyenoord 40:256
Fynd 40:227-8
Gael 39:154
Galila 38:93
Gandy 37:6
Gansey 39:155
Gardar Thorsteinsson (trawler) 39:160
Garvelpark 37:59
Gaspard 37:10
Gatchina 39:139
Gatling 39:151
Gay Med 39:141
Gaza 39:163
Gemma 38:77;40:233
General Belgrano 38:92
General George Brink 40:231
General Mola (submarine) 37:48
General Sanjurio

(submarine) 39:132
General Sikorski 39:163
Generton 40:257
Genesee 37:44
George (1949) 38:97
George (1954) 37:30
George Washington 37:59
Georgios S. 38:70
Georgy 37:30
Gerit (tug) 40:215
Germania 38:76
Gertie (1902) 37:40
Gertor 37:60
Gesine P 39:186
Gianandrea 40:196
Gilbertson (dredger) 38:103
Gipsy Queen 38:106
Gitana 38:70
Gladonia (1963) 37:15,17
Gladstone (tug) 40:217
Gladstone Star 39:173,179
Glanmire 39:158
Glasgow 37:21
Glebula 39:163
Gledburn 39:142-3
Glen Rosa 38:106
Glenaffric 40:251
Glenapp 39:180-1
Glenaray 39:154
Glenbeg 38:110
Glenclune 39:165
Gleniffer 40:256
Glenstal 40:229
Global Carrier 38:101
Glodale 40:260
Gneisenau 39:139
Goddess (yacht) 38:106
Golden City 39:179
Golden Future 37:10
Golden Madonna 39:173
Golden Princess 39:174
Good Hope Castle 39:174
Gothic Star 40:248-9
Gothicstar 40:248-9
Gower (tug) 37:43
Grab Hopper Barge No.1 38:111
Grab Hopper No. 1 37:36
Grab Hopper No. 2 37:36
Grace Dollar 37:43
Grace Gibson 37:45
Graceful 39:185
Grada Westers 39:186
Graf Stroganoff 37:43
Grampus 37:46
Grand Michael 40:206
Grangetoft 39:142-4
Grayotter (tug) 40:218
Grebe 40:196
Greenport 37:22;38:83
Grenville 38:114
Griqua 40:228
Gudruda (yacht) 38:106
Gulf Reliance 38:117
Gutenfels 38:119
GWC No 11 37:12
GWC No 12 37:12
Hadar 38:93,97
Hadiotis 37:57
Haflidi (trawler) 39:160
Hai Ji Shun 37:10
Halifax Star 39:174
Hampton Ferry 39:146
Hanan 38:76
Hanan Star 38:76
Hannah 37:48
Harald Schröder 37:47
Haraldawins 37:6
Hare 37:48
Harebell (HMS) 38:105
Harelda 37:6
Harpoon 38:113
Hatasu 39:139
Hawkins (HMS) 38:107
Hazel Dollar 40:233-4
Hazelgarth (tug) 40:218
He Ping 28 37:10
Heath Cock (tug) 40:217
Hecla (HMS) 39:186
Heelsum 38:119
Heleanna 37:60
Helen Heidmann 40:226

Hellas (tug) 40:217
Henry Foss (tug) 39:190
Herakles (tug) 40:215
Heraklion 37:60
Herborg 40:253
Hermes 37:10
Hermiston 40:257
Heron 40:206
Hibernia(tug) 40:214
Hie Khean 37:10
Highland Fling 39:170-1
Highland Laddie 38:103
Highland Monarch 37:49,52;38:111
Hindustan 38:116
Hirondelle 40:205
Hobart Star 39:173
Holderness 39:134,142-4
Holdernett 39:142
Holmia 38:73
Homeford 40:230
Hong Bo 3 37:10
Hong Xiang 37:10
Hopeful 39:185
Hopper No.7 39:156
Hopper No.10 39:159
Hornby (tug) 39:157
HS 45 (tug) 37:11
Hubert 39:174
Hudson Firth 39:160
Hun Jiang 37:10
Huntington (USS) 37:59
Huntsend 40:257
Huntsgreen 40:257
Hyang Ro Bong 37:10
Hyrcania 39:149
I-25 39:190,192
I-26 39:190
I-27 39:191-2
I-124 37:6
Ibadan Palm 37:56
Iberian 37:45
Ilion 38:101
Ilorin 39:135
Ilorin Palm 37:56
Imber (1914) 37:5,8-9; 38:82
Imber (1920) 38:68-9
Imperial Star 39:172-3
Import 37:47
Inca 39:154
Indefatigable (HMS) 37:50;38:110
Indomitable (HMS) 38:107
Inniscroone 40:234
Integrity 37:15
Invercloy 39:156
Iona 38:103
Ionian 39:134
Irenes Banner 38:120;39:185
Iris (1954) 37:30
Irk (dredger) 39:155;37:33,36
Ironsider (tug) 40:219
Iroquois 38:107
Irwell (dredger) 38:84
Isabena 40:232
Islay Trader 37:19
Isle of Harris 39:186
Italcielo 37:22
Ithaca Star 39:164
Itsukushima Maru 39:169
J.D. Hazen 38:105
J.O. Gravel (tug) 37:11,34
Ja Gang 37:10
Jabiru 37:2,8
Jacinth 39:158
Jack Wharton 37:17
Jah 38:100
Jaipur 37:10
Jamaica (HMS) 38:112
Jamaica Settler 38:103
James Lamey (tug) 39:157
Janus (HMS) 37:8
Jat Na Mu 37:10
Jean Baptiste 39:168
Jeanne D'Arc 37:43
Jednosc Robotnicza 39:163
Jef de Smedt 38:77
Jervis (HMS) 37:8
Jin Da Hai 37:10
Jing Ren 37:10

Johanna 39:169
John Coulson (tug) 38:105
John M. Palmer 40:231
John Perring 39:152
Jokob Ekkenga (trawler) 39:159
Juno 39:139
Kaapland 40:232
Kabala 38:83
Kabala 38:121
Kanhaiya (tug) 40:218
Kana 39:141
Kanaris 38:121
Kalewa 39:162
Kalalamba 38:102
Kantara (1925) 39:129,139
Kantara (1947) 38:119;40:198
Karapiperis 10 (tug) 40:214
Karapiperis III (tug) 40:215
Kardamila 37:39
Karnak 40:197-8,200,206,210
Kassos 37:57
Kastriani III 40:201,211
Kastro K 37:30
Kate (1952) 37:24;40:204
Kate A 38:118
Kathlamba 38:102
Katia 37:24;40:204
Kaupanger 37:42
Kavak 39:141
Kavo Astrapi 39:179
Kavo Peiratis 38:119;39:161
Kenia 39:152
Kerkennah 38:126
Keta Lagoon 38:95,101
Khalij Crystal 39:178
Khandalla 38:109
Khedive Ismail 39:192
Kheti 39:140-1;40:197
Kien Loong 38:75
Kilgarth (tug) 40:217
Kilkenny 39:160
Killygordon (HMS) 40:230
Kilmore (tug) 40:217
King Alexandra 38:121
King Alfred 39:182
King Arthur 38:121
King George V (HMS) 37:49-50;38:110
King Malcolm 38:121
Kingsnorth Fisher 37:31
Kirkham (barge) 38:104
Kirkwynd 39:135
Kittiwake (1919) 38:67,69-71
Kittiwake (1945) 38:76-8
Klorte Lagoon 38:100
Korle Lagoon 38:94,98
Kronos I 38:115
Kronos II 38:115
Ku Ryong 37:10
Kufra (1929) 39:140-1;40:197
Kufra (1937) 40:206
Kulpawn River 38:98
Kum Gang 37:10
Kumara 40:257
Kyle Castle 37:3
Kyleglen 39:137
Kypros 40:203-4,206,212
Kyrenia 40:195
L.21 (HMS) 38:105
L.69 (HMS) 38:105
L'Avenir (barque) 39:189
La Sierra 38:115
Lady Gwendolen 37:28
Lady Hyacinth 39:186
Lady L'Belle 37:25
Lady Lotmore 37:25
Lady of Mann 39:160
Lady Sylvia 38:115
Laeveld 40:230
Lafian 40:195
Lagosian 37:56-7;39:183;40:233
Lairdsbank 39:158
Lairdsloch 38:104
Lake 40:223
Lake Bosomtwe 38:94,98
Lake Champlain 38:107
Lanarkshire (1871) 39:129,165,168

Lanarkshire (1940) **40**:243
Landes **39**:138-9;**40**:205
Lasia **38**:120
Lato **39**:164
Laurentic **39**:178
Lena **39**:163
Leon (tug) **40**:215
Lestris (1921)
    38:70-1;**39**:184
Lestris (1946) **38**:76-7
Leviathan **37**:59
Li Jia **37**:10
Lian **38**:123
Libra Star **38**:101
Liby **40**:195
Lien **39**:186
Lillöhus **37**:29
Lily Royal **37**:10
Limelight **39**:158
Limoges **40**:194
Limon **40**:255
Lingeborg **37**:25
Lingestroom **40**:228
Linkmoor **37**:22
Lion **38**:101
Lisa L **37**:10
Liverpool **38**:70
Livonia **39**:142
Lizzonia (1980) **37**:15,17-8
Loch Broom **40**:236
Loch Etive **37**:59;**38**:82
Loch Frisa **38**:83;**40**:236
Loch Ryan **37**:26
Lochbroom **38**:82-3;**39**:184
Lochfyne **39**:160
Lock Veyatie (HMS) **39**:155
Lommaren **39**:164
Long Fu **37**:10
Loradore **38**:120
Lord Anson (drifter) **38**:112
Lord Gladstone **40**:235
Lormont (1920) **39**:138-9
Lormont (1927) **40**:197
Lormont (1930) **40**:205
Los Teques **40**:207
Lublin **40**:196
Lucerne **39**:151
Lucullite **38**:103
Ludgate (tug) **37**:49
Lugano **39**:160;**40**:247
Lundoge **37**:10
Lupin (HMS) **40**:243,250
Lützow **40**:257
Lycaon **40**:256
Lyng **39**:142
M.E. Dollar **39**:184
M.O.B. (barge) **39**:156
Maashaven **39**:152
Macbeth (trawler) **39**:155
Macedonia **38**:104
Madge **39**:156
Magicstar **40**:245-6
Magnetic **38**:102
Magneticlight **38**:102
Magnolia **38**:110
Mahana **38**:109;**39**:188
Mahsuri **38**:86-7,92;**39**:174
(Maindy Cottage) **39**:142
Maindy Keep **39**:142
Maindy Tower **39**:142-3
Maindy Transport **39**:142
Mairoula **38**:74;**39**:133
Makaria **40**:206-7,213
Makeni Palm **38**:122,126
Makurdi Palm **38**:122,125
Malay Star **38**:86;**39**:174
Malay **38**:86;**39**:174
Malaysia **39**:174
Malcolm (HMS) **38**:72
Maldive Express **38**:80
Maltese Princess **38**:84
Man Pung **37**:10
Manchester City (1937) **37**:25
Manchester Explorer **37**:3
Manchester Importer **37**:46
Manchester Regiment
    39:182
Manchester Trader (1890)
    37:42
Mandama **38**:86-7,92
Mania **38**:77
Manipur (HMS) **38**:106-7

Marauder (tug) **37**:50
Marcellus **39**:169
Marco **38**:128;**40**:257
Marco Polo **37**:60
Mardina Importer
    37:54;**39**:161
Margam (tug) **40**:220
Maria B **37**:27
Maria C **38**:118
Maria K **38**:118
Marichu **39**:136
Marietta Ralli **37**:61
Marigold (HMS) **40**:194
Mario Piro **39**:141
Marion Merrett **39**:135
Marleen **38**:83
Marloch **37**:8
Maroulio **39**:137
Marsdale **38**:93,96
Marsh Cock (tug) **39**:157
Martin Oldfield (tug) **37**:34
Marton Cross (tug) **40**:220
Mary Kingsley **40**:234
Mashona Coast **40**:231
Masterman (tug) **38**:107
Matadi **38**:123
Matadi Palm (1948)
    38:65;**38**:122-5
Matadi Palm (1970)
    38:122-3
Matadian (1936) **38**:122-3
Matadian (1948) **38**:122-5
Matje **38**:103
Mavis **37**:7
Mayfair **38**:114
Mayon II **38**:97
Mead **40**:230
Med Star **39**:141
Mediterranean Sea **39**:147
Medlock (dredger) **37**:33
Megalochari VII (tug)
    40:216
Megalochari XII (tug)
    40:219
Melic Sun **38**:115
Melita **40**:193,206-7,213
Mellite **39**:158
Melmay
    37:56;**39**:183-4;**40**:233-4
Memphis (1909) **39**:132-3
Memphis (1947) **40**:
    197-9,209
Menelaus **38**:109
Mercator **40**:259
Merchantman (tug) **38**:108
Meremba **40**:258
Merganser (1919) **38**:67-8
Merganser (1946)
    37:4-5;**38**:77-8;**40**:233
Meroe **39**:131;**40**:195
Meropi **38**:104
Mersey (dredger) **38**:84
Mersey No. 37 (barge)
    39:157
Meziane **39**:132
Mien An **40**:195
Mike **38**:70
Mikula Seleaninovitch
    38:105
Mikula **38**:105
Milos E **38**:100
Milos F **38**:100
Milwaukee **37**:50;**38**:107
Mimiro **40**:257
Mimis N. Papalios **37**:58
Minnekahda **37**:49;**38**:103
Minos **37**:60
Minotavros (tug)**40**:215,219
Minoutsi **38**:119-20
Miranda Guinness **37**:28
Mohawk (HMS) **37**:8
Mokoia **40**:240
Molly (barge) **38**:103
Mona Lisa **40**:254
Moncenisio **37**:41
Monowai **40**:240
Montcalm **38**:109
Monte Cristo **39**:168
Monte **37**:10
(Montrose) **40**:201
Morayshire (1890)
    39:166-7,170-1

Morayshire (1898)
    40:239,241,247
Morgenster **40**:232
Mormaclake **40**:223
Mormacpride **40**:223
Moyles **40**:234
Mozart **38**:102
MSC Archer (tug)
    37:26,54; **38**:83; **39**:157
MSC Arrow (tug) **38**:83
MSC Bollin **37**:34
MSC Dainty (tug) **37**:36
MSC Daphne (tug) **37**:36
MSC Daring (tug) **37**:36
MSC Dart **37**:36;**38**:84
MSC Dawn (tug) **37**:35
MSC Deborah (tug) **37**:36
MSC Delta (barge)
    37:12,34-5
MSC Diana (tug) **37**:35
MSC Dido (tug) **37**:36
MSC Firefly (tug) **37**:27
MSC Gamma (barge)
    37:12,34-5
MSC Gowy (dredger)
    37:34,36
MSC Ince (dredger)
    37:32,36
MSC Irwell (dredger)
    37:32,36
Munsterland **39**:162
Murell **39**:186
Murray (HMS) **39**:159
Mushtari (1917) **37**:58-9
Mushtari (1942) **37**:58
Myra Fell **40**:260
N.O. Petersen **39**:186
Nailsea Moor **38**:105
Nailsea Tower **38**:105
Nailsea Vale **38**:105
Nairnshire (1889)**39**:166-70
Nairnshire (1899)
    40:239,241,248-9
Nakwa River **38**:94,100
Nama **37**:10
Nanking **37**:10
Nasia River **38**:97
Natal Coast **40**:229
Nausika **38**:65
Naval Gent **37**:10
Naya **38**:114
Nemeo **37**:23
Neptune Star **40**:225,229
Nestor (1913) **40**:251
Nestor (1952) **40**:251
Netherhall (tug) **38**:104
Netty **39**:186
New Bern Victory **40**:232
New Gen **37**:31
New Generation **37**:31
New Jersey (USS) **37**:59
New Legend Star **37**:10
New Pioneer **40**:234
New York **37**:50;**38**:108
New York Star **39**:174
Newcastle Star **39**:173
Niagara **39**:187
Niceto **37**:38
Nicola **37**:21
Nigerian **40**:195
Nikolaos S **37**:10
Nilos **38**:102
Nisos Kalymnos (tug)
    40:214
Ni-Tricia **39**:187
Nitsa **39**:191
No. 37 (barge) **39**:157
Noemi **40**:235
Nomadisch **39**:186
Nong Gong Shan 8 **37**:10
Norbrit Faith **37**:16
Nordana **37**:10
Nordanbris **38**:110
Nordmark **38**:110
Nordwind **38**:120
Norge **40**:257
North Cock (tug) **39**:157
North Eastern **37**:46
North Western **40**:234
Northern Chief **40**:240
Northmark **38**:110
Northumberland **39**:179

Norwalk Victory **38**:77
Notos **38**:97
Novanoor **37**:58
Nubian (HMS) **37**:8
Nyassa **40**:257
Nyroca (1903) **37**:5,7
Nyroca (1917) **38**:74;**39**:133
Ocean (HMS) **39**:184
Ocean Endurance **37**:58
Ocean Ensign **37**:59
Ocean Pilgrim **37**:60
Ocean Princess **38**:79
Offin River **38**:97
Okishima Maru **39**:185
Olaf **37**:38
Old Lochfyne **39**:160
Old Oak **39**:141
Old Quay (tug) **37**:38
Olga Minacoulis **40**:235
Olga S **40**:227
Olwen **37**:58
Olympia **39**:184
Omoa **37**:54;**39**:161
Ondo **37**:27
Opobo Palm **38**:122-4
Oranaise **37**:8
Orduña **37**:50;**38**:108-9
Orestes **40**:251
Oriana **38**:90
Orica **39**:161
Oriental Kiku **37**:10
Orion **38**:93
Ormonde **37**:49;**38**:109
Ormos **40**:230
Osmond **37**:43
Otchi River **38**:97
Oti River **38**:99
Oti **37**:27
Ottawa Maycliff
    38:83;**40**:236
Ousel **37**:4;**38**:70-2;**39**:184
Ovingdean Grange **40**:235
P.M. Cooper (barge) **39**:157
Pacific Envoy **37**:26
Pacific Reliance **37**:26
Pajala **39**:164
Palau **38**:126
Palo Duro **38**:113
Panaghia Tinou **40**:230
Pandion **37**:3;**38**:72,74
Pangani **37**:10
Papanui **39**:178
Paparoa **39**:178
Paraskevi H **39**:185
Parkmore **37**:42
Paros **37**:28
Parthia **38**:83
Partridge **38**:104
Pass of Balmaha **39**:156
Pati **38**:118
Patonga **39**:178
Patrician **40**:239
Patriot State **40**:223
Patterson (USS) **39**:192
Pavonis **37**:10
Peakdale (dredger)
    37:34;**39**:159
Pegasus (HMS) **37**:63
Pembroke Coast **38**:104
Penguin **38**:104
Penny Transoceanic **39**:163
Pentland **37**:17
Peramataris **38**:117-8
Pericles **39**:169
Perim **39**:178
Persia **38**:88
Perthshire **40**:238-45
Petard (HMS) **39**:192
Peterjohn **37**:57
Petit Folmer **39**:187
(Petite Fulmar) **39**:187
Philine **39**:161
Philosopher **38**:83
Philotis (1917)**38**:74;**39**:133
Philotis (1926) **40**:196
Phloisvos **39**:136
Photinia **37**:31;**40**:235-6
Phuc Hai **37**:10
Phuong Dong 01 **37**:10
Phuong Dong 02 **37**:10
Phuong Dong 03 **37**:10

Pia Stevns **37**:19
Pial **39**:186
Pibroch **39**:156,189
Pilarella **40**:205
Pinemore **38**:84
Pinewood (barge) **39**:164
Ping Jiang **37**:10
Pinguin **39**:176
Pino **39**:168
Pipiriki **39**:178
Plainsman **38**:83
Plassy **37**:57-8
Plettenberg **40**:226
Plover (barge) **38**:111
Plumgarth (tug) **40**:215
Pluto (HMS) **39**:160
Poland **37**:8
Polar Chief **38**:109
Polar Paraguay **40**:254
Polgowan **38**:104
Polikos (tug) **40**:219
Politician **37**:50
Pollux **38**:110
Pontiac **37**:46
Port Chalmers **40**:225
Port Hacking **40**:257
Port Hobart **39**:176
Port Launay **39**:178
Port Launceston **39**:177
Port Napier **39**:176
Port Pirie **39**:176
Port St. Lawrence **40**:255
Port Sydney **39**:174
Port Wellington **39**:176
Portadown **38**:103
Portland **37**:19
Portway **39**:159
Poseidon II (tug) **40**:219
Poseidon III (tug) **40**:215
Potosi **38**:119;**39**:161
Powell **39**:162
Powhatan **37**:59
Pra River **38**:94,97
Premier Atlantic **38**:117
President Coolidge **39**:184
President Harding **39**:184
President Kruger **40**:231
President Reitz **40**:231
President Steyn **40**:231
Presidente Ramon S Castillo
    37:10
Pressman (tug) **39**:153
Pretoria Castle **40**:225
Pride **40**:223
Prince Ja Ja **38**:103
Prinsdal **40**:254
Prinses Juliana (dredger)
    37:33-5;**39**:159
Prinz Oskar **38**:93
Procris **39**:135
Procyon **38**:120;**39**:186
Psara **38**:96
Pstrowski **39**:163
Pullwell (tug) **40**:219
Pussur **37**:58
Q.26 **37**:7
Q.34 **37**:6
Qing Jiang **37**:10
QSM Dubai **37**:10
Queda **40**:234
Queen Elizabeth (HMS)
    37:50-1;**38**:107
Queen Frederica **37**:60
Queen Mary (1935) **39**:184
Queen of the Mersey (tug)
    37:44
Quesnel (HMCS) **39**:190
Quiros **37**:43
R.B. Telford **37**:55
Ra Nam **37**:10
Radiant (yacht) **37**:57
Raima **39**:163
Rakaia **37**:58;**38**:83
Rallus **37**:1;**38**:70-1;**39**:184
Rapid **39**:186
Reef **38**:75
Reefer City **40**:255
Reefer Princess **39**:179
(Regal) **39**:164
Regent Spirit **37**:60
Regina **38**:107
Reina del Mar **37**:61

264